THE CASE FOR ERNST LOHMEYER

Also by J.W. Rogerson

Cultural Landscapes and the Bible:
Collected Essays (2015)

The Kingdom of God:
Five Lectures (2015)

The Holy Spirit in Biblical and
Pastoral Perspective (2013)

Perspectives on the Passion (2014)

On Being a Broad Church:
An Exploration (2013)

Published by Beauchief Abbey Press
and available from www.lulu.com

The Case for
Ernst Lohmeyer

J. W. Rogerson

BEAUCHIEF
ABBEY·PRESS

Published by Beauchief Abbey Press, Beauchief Abbey, Beauchief
Abbey Lane, Sheffield S8 9EL, February 2016

www.beauchiefabbeypress.co.uk

Copyright © J W Rogerson, 2016
The author asserts his moral right under the Copyright, Designs and
Patents Act, 1988, to be identified as the author of this work.

Scripture quotations from the Authorized (King James) Version.
Rights in the Authorized Version in the United Kingdom are vested
in the Crown. Reproduced by permission of the Crown's patentee,
Cambridge University Press

ISBN: 978-0-9935499-4-6

A CIP catalogue record for this title is available from the British
Library.

Cover design by Michael Lindley, Truth Studio, Studio 15, Sum
Studios, 1 Hartley Street, Sheffield S2 3AQ. www.truthstudio.co.uk

Printed by www.lulu.com

Contents

Foreword

I am once again grateful to Beauchief Abbey Press for accepting and publishing a book that no commercial publisher would be likely to take on. I am also grateful to Mary Hodge for formatting and sub-editing the text.

John Birtwhistle kindly lent me, on long loan, the English translation of the poems of Stefan George, while the University Library in Wrocław provided a copy of the address delivered by Lohmeyer as Rector of the University of Breslau in 1930/31.

I hope, at the very least, that a few English-speaking readers will come to appreciate the genius of Ernst Lohmeyer. While, in an ideal world, it would be good if some of his work could be translated (the same goes for his colleague Richard Hönigswald), this is unlikely to happen. What is offered here will hopefully be a very small contribution to filling a very large gap.

J. W. Rogerson
Sheffield, January 2016

Ernst Johannes Lohmeyer

Introduction

I first came across Ernst Lohmeyer over forty-five years ago. I was writing one of the final chapters for my book on myth in the interpretation of the Old Testament, when I discussed briefly the debate in the 1940s engendered by Rudolf Bultmann's essay on demythologising.[1] In the English translation of the symposium that this debate generated, I found a contribution by Ernst Lohmeyer on the correct understanding of the mythical. I was very impressed by this essay, because it was concerned to try to understand rather than to deconstruct the idea of myth, and I wondered who he was, especially as he had delivered this lecture in 1944.[2]

At about the same time, in my work as an Anglican priest, which involved me in taking services on Sundays in addition to my full-time job as a university teacher, I had regularly to preach on passages from Matthew's Gospel which were set in the Book of Common Prayer as the Gospel for many Sundays. There were not many commentaries on Matthew available at that time, but among those that were available was one by Ernst Lohmeyer. It was incomplete, because the author had begun to write it just before the Second World War and had had to continue his work during that war while serving as an officer on the eastern front. His tragic death in 1946 had left the commentary unfinished. It was published in 1956 by one

---

[1] J. W. Rogerson, *Myth in Old Testament Interpretation* (Beihefte zur Zeitschrift für die alttestamentliche Wissenschaft (BZAW), 134) Berlin: De Gruyter, 1974.

[2] E. Lohmeyer, 'The Right Interpretation of the Mythical' in H. W. Bartsch, *Kerygma and Myth. A Theological Debate* (translated by R. H. Fuller), London: SPCK, 1964, pp.124-136. Bultmann's essay, which sparked off the controversy, is given on pp.1-44. For further, fuller details see p.175.

of his pupils, who in some cases was able to add material from notes left by Lohmeyer.

This commentary quickly became my favourite and my main point of reference for preparing sermons on passages from Matthew's Gospel. Although it was not always easy to get through the long paragraphs in small print and dense thought that accompanied the more usual historical critical paragraphs in larger print, I was constantly surprised by the depth of insight that Lohmeyer was able to bring out of the biblical passages without indulging in any theological special pleading. For good or ill, many of the sermons that I preached in the 1970s owed not a little to Lohmeyer.

I remember a conversation with my Durham New Testament colleague and friend, C. K. Barrett, on the subject of Lohmeyer. He told me that Lohmeyer had been elected Rector of the University of Greifswald in 1945, and that on the eve of the reopening of the university in February 1946 he had been arrested by the Soviet authorities (Greifswald was in the Russian Occupation Zone) and had later been executed by them. Fortunately, the Durham University Library possessed the memorial volume to Lohmeyer, published in 1951, and I was able to learn a little more about him. A photograph of him between pages 16 and 18 portrayed a formidable looking man with eyes intensely focused, presumably on the camera before him. Kingsley Barrett and I both agreed that he was not the kind of person that one would have wanted to disagree with.

With the publication of the Alternative Service Book by the Church of England in 1980, the traditional Gospels for particular Sundays were replaced by a wider variety of set passages, and Matthew's Gospel lost its predominant position. It had owed this, in the Book of Common Prayer, to the belief of the pre-Reformation Western Church that Matthew's was an eyewitness gospel (Matthew was identified with Levi the tax collector in Matthew 9.9 and Mark 2.14), and the first, and fullest gospel to be written. My need for Lohmeyer's Matthew commentary became less great, and he receded into the background of my life. My interest in him was revived by the publication in 2004 of an excellent biographical study by Andreas Köhn, and indeed the present book is deeply indebted to his work.[3] Of particular interest was the fact that Lohmeyer had been influenced by the philosopher Richard Hönigswald – a scholar whose name was not known to me – and by the poet Stefan George whose name was familiar to me only because I knew that a member of the George circle, Claus Graf von Stauffenberg, had tried unsuccessfully to assassinate Adolf Hitler in July 1944.

My interest in the possible philosophical influences upon Lohmeyer was fuelled by my own conviction that Biblical Studies cannot adequately be carried out without a knowledge of philosophy and an awareness of one's own philosophical commitments. People who deny this are, in my opinion, unaware of their own philosophical positions and how that may affect their biblical scholarship. In my biography of W.M.L. de Wette, I devoted a good deal of space to the importance of J.F. Fries's post-Kantian philosophy for de Wette's work; and earlier, in my study of Old Testament criticism in Britain and Germany in the nineteeth century, I had argued that the different paths taken by critical scholarship in those two countries resulted from the differing philosophical traditions underlying the theology of the Lutheran and Anglican churches.

---

[3] A. Köhn, *Der Neutestamentler Ernst Lohmeyer. Studien zu Biographie und Theologie.* (Wissenschaftliche Untersuchungen zum Neuen Testament 2), Reihe 180, Tübingen: Mohr Siebeck, 2004.

From Köhn's study I discovered that Hönigwald's influence on Lohmeyer was so profound that some of his contemporaries, in particular Hans Lietzmann, claimed not to be able to make any sense of what Lohmeyer was writing, and that his work was wholly unrepresentative of German New Testament scholarship. Köhn's book also answered a question that had long been in my mind from my days of using Lohmeyer's Matthew commentary for sermons, and that was why the adjective 'eschatological' was used so frequently by Lohmeyer. It became apparent from Köhn that Lohmeyer's understanding of eschatology was closely bound up with Hönigswald's view of time, which in its turn was embedded in his complicated theories of perception and experience, and their implications for the nature of reality. All this has led me into a study of Hönigswald and into a very unfamiliar area of philosophy. What I think I have understood of it has been illuminating. Also, I have tried to get to grips with Stefan George, and this in turn has taken me back to Hölderlin, who was so important for Lohmeyer, as also for George.

The death of Lohmeyer in 1946 at the age of only 56 meant that his influence on New Testament study was cut brutally short, and that it was the students of Rudolf Bultmann who came to dominate the scholarship of the post-war period.

What would have happened if Lohmeyer had been spared to work for, say, another 15 years cannot, of course be said. The publication of Köhn's biographical study indicates that he has not been entirely forgotten; and about the same time as the publication of Köhn's book there appeared a study of Lohmeyer by Dieter Kuhn.[4] This is less valuable than Köhn's book, although it does serve to supplement it in some

---

[4] D. Kuhn, *Metaphysik und Geschichte. Zur Theologie Ernst Lohmeyers.* (Theologische Bibliothek Töpelmann, 131), Berlin: De Gruyter, 2005.

important respects. It is also interesting that Eberhard Jüngel devoted some space to Lohmeyer's understanding of the parables of Jesus in his *Paulus und Jesus*.[5]

I am not a New Testament scholar, but as far as I am aware little attention has been paid to Lohmeyer in the English-speaking world. Little of his work is available in English translation, the best known being his study of the Lord's Prayer. New Testament colleagues in Britain are surprised to learn that Lohmeyer was writing about the sociology of the early Christian movement in the 1920s, 50 years before this became fashionable in North America and Europe, and that he drew attention to the importance of Galilee for understanding Jesus as early as 1936 in his *Galiläa und Jerusalem*.

The purpose of the present book is to try to persuade readers in the English speaking world to reconsider Lohmeyer's work, and especially the particular philosophical thinking that characterised it. That I am indebted to earlier scholars, particularly Köhn, goes without saying. However, I have tried to undertake an independent study of Hönigswald and George, not to mention Lohmeyer himself. This has not been easy, as I am now physically less able to visit Germany in order to spend appropriate amounts of time in German libraries. The Internet has enabled me to purchase the great majority of Lohmeyer's main works; but I have not read everything that he wrote, and this is obviously a weakness, although hopefully not a fatal one.

Because this book is intended for English speaking readers, most of whom will be unfamiliar with the philosophical scene

---

[5] E. Jüngel, *Paulus und Jesus. Eine Untersuchung zur Präzisierung der Frage nach dem Ursprung der Christologie* (Hermeneutische Untersuchungen zur Theologie 2), Tübingen: Mohr Siebeck, 2004 (7th ed.), pp.120-127

in Germany in the early part of the twentieth century, it will be necessary to write at a more elementary level than if a German readership were being addressed. The need for greater simplicity will not, hopefully, mean a loss of profundity.

Lohmeyer's Life and Career:
A Brief Outline

Ernst Johannes Lohmeyer was born on 8 July 1890 in Dorsten, a small town on the northern edge of the Ruhr area and some 16 miles to the east of the river Rhine. His father was the protestant minister there. In 1895 his father moved to Vlotho on the River Weser in the proximity of Herford, and it was in the Herford *Gymnasium* that Lohmeyer received his primary and secondary education. In 1908 he enrolled in the University of Tübingen to study theology, philosophy and oriental languages (Aramaic and Accadian). However, by the winter semester of 1909 he was in Berlin, where among his teachers were K. L. Schmidt, Adolf Deissmann and Martin Dibelius. He gained his doctorate in July 1912 on the subject of *Diatheke* (Covenant), and his first theological state examination was completed in the December of the same year.

On 1 October 1913 Lohmeyer became a volunteer in the Seventh Westphalian Cavalry regiment, which brought him to military service in the First World War. In July 1916 he married Mellie Seyberth. Without being in any sense a militarist, Lohmeyer seems to have shared the general view of his young contemporaries that it was a duty to fight for one's country and to defend its cultural heritage. During his military service he displayed that total commitment to his academic work that characterised his turbulent life. A philosophical dissertation on Anselm of Canterbury's Doctrine of the Will was defended in Erlangen in January 1914 and a *Habilitation* was defended in Heidelberg in October 1918. On 1 December

1918, Lohmeyer was appointed as a *Privatdozent* for New Testament in Heidelberg. It was during this period in Heidelberg that he almost certainly came into contact with the circle around Stefan George.

After two years in Heidelberg, Lohmeyer moved to Breslau as an *ausserordentlicher* professor in October 1920, and on 1 February 1921 he became a full tenured professor. He was to remain in Breslau, the second most important city in Prussia, until his enforced removal to Greifswald in 1935 by the National Socialist Régime. In Breslau he found among his colleagues Richard Hönigswald, who had been connected with Breslau since 1906 and in 1919 had been appointed to a full professorship for philosophy, psychology and pedagogy. Hönigswald was some 15 years older than Lohmeyer; the influence of the older philosopher on the younger theologian played a decisive role in Lohmeyer's life and work. Their close friendship continued after Hönigswald's move to Munich in 1930, his enforced retirement because of his Jewish ancestry in 1933, and his emigration to the United States via Switzerland in 1939.

Lohmeyer's main writings in his Breslau period included his commentaries on the Book of Revelation (1926), Philippians (1928), Colossians and Philemon (1930), and two philosophical and theological works, *Vom Begriff der religiösen Gemeinschaft* (1928) and *Grundlagen paulinischer Theologie* (1929). In 1932, Lohmeyer published the first and only instalment of what was intended to be a multi-volume project on Early Christianity. It dealt with John the Baptist. In 1930-31, he served as Rector of the University of Breslau.

The rise of National Socialism and the activities of National Socialist and German Christian student organisations impinged significantly on Lohmeyer's work in Breslau. He was actively opposed to Nazi student attempts to boycott and disrupt the lectures of the Jewish law lecturer Ernst Cohn; and in his office as director of the theological seminary, he banned two articles in the Nazi organ, the *Völkischer Beobachter*, directed against the Tübingen Catholic theologian Karl Adam. In 1933 he wrote an open letter of support to the Jewish philosopher Martin Buber; and was one of 21 New Testament scholars who signed the declaration of the Marburg theological faculty, denouncing the decision of the synod of the Evangelical Church of the Old Prussian Union to carry out the provisions of the Aryan Clauses of 1933. These required the dismissal of any minister or other church office holder of Jewish descent. In 1934 Lohmeyer joined the Confessing Church, the opposition church movement whose basis was the Barmen Confession drawn up in May 1934. Because of his unconcealed hostility to the National Socialist Régime, Lohmeyer was forcibly removed from his prestigious chair in Breslau to the comparatively unimportant but small and ancient University of Greifswald in 1935. In 1936 there appeared his *Galiläa und Jerusalem* and in 1937 his commentary on Mark's Gospel.

On the outbreak of the Second World War, Lohmeyer was conscripted at the age of 49 as an officer and served for four years, initially in Poland, then in Bavaria, the Netherlands, France and Belgium and, finally, on the eastern front in the Ukraine. He worked tirelessly to maintain standards of decency and also continued his academic work, especially his commentary on Matthew's Gospel. He also published *Kultus und Evangelium* (1942). In November 1943 he was released from military service and was able to return to Greifswald. It was thanks to this that he was able to deliver his lecture on the demythologising debate in January 1944.

Lohmeyer was one of the small group of citizens who, in defiance of Hitler's 'destroy everything' order, surrendered the city of Greifswald to the Soviet Army on 30 April 1945, in order to spare it and its citizens from destruction. Lohmeyer was appointed Rector of the university, and began to work for its reopening. This was due to take place on 16 February 1946, but on the evening of 15 February, Lohmeyer was arrested by the Soviet authorities. His exact fate was not known for many years, and it was only after the collapse of the Soviet Union in 1990 that it became known for certain that he had been executed on 19 September 1946. On 15 August 1996 he was posthumously rehabilitated by the Russian Federation.

There seem to have been a number of reasons for Lohmeyer's arrest and murder. Various false charges had been made against him by German Communists: for example, that he had been involved in the mass shooting by the Gestapo at Bydgoszcz in Poland and those in Bromberg.[6] Again, it was thought by some that Lohmeyer had not been sufficiently thorough in dismissing from the academic staff in Greifswald those who had been Nazi party members. Apparently, one reason for Lohmeyer's reluctance to dismiss party members was his fear that the weakened physical condition of the civilians and the shortage of food and fuel would lead to an outbreak of infectious diseases, and he did not want the medical faculty to be non-existent if this proved to be the case.

Whatever the true reasons, the execution of Lohmeyer was a tragedy for theological scholarship, not to mention for his family and friends.

---

[6] Köhn, *Lohmeyer*, p.104, note 2

CHAPTER ONE

Richard Hönigswald

Richard Hönigswald was born on 18 July 1875 in what is now Mosonmagyaróvár in Hungary, some 10 miles east of the border with Austria and around 40 miles due south of Bratislava. He attended the *Gymnasium* in what is today Györ, some 25 miles southeast of his birth-place, and in 1892 he enrolled at the University of Vienna, some 50 miles to the northwest of his birthplace, to study medicine. His parents were Jewish and his father a medical doctor. In November 1904 he was baptised into the Protestant Reformed Church.

It seems to have been the influence of Hönigswald's father that determined his decision to study medicine, and he was awarded his Dr. med. degree in March 1902. However, his real interest lay elsewhere, and in May 1902 he enrolled at the University of Halle-Wittenberg in order to study mainly philosophy. He gained a Dr. phil. in Halle in July 1904, but continued his philosophical studies at the University of Graz. In August 1906 he moved to Breslau, and in October of the same year defended his *Habilitation* dissertation under the title of *Beiträge zur Erkenntnisthorie und Methodenlehre*. This gave him the right to lecture in the philosophical faculty.

Having qualified in medicine, Hönigswald never practised as a medical doctor. However, his medical studies played an important part in his intellectual development, a factor that has been exhaustively researched by Roswitha Grassl.[7] The medical faculty in Vienna during Hönigswald's student years was distinguished by its attention to and achievements in medicine as an empirical, experimental scientific discipline. To some, however, including Hönigswald, this approach seemed to treat human beings as physical or chemical objects to the exclusion of everything else. According to this, all illnesses and disorders could be described and treated in physical causal ways. One scholar who attracted Hönigswald's attention was the biologist Hans Driesch (1867-1941), whose research on sea urchins showed that a single cell taken from an embryo could develop into a full sea urchin. There was therefore an internal structuring principle within cells, particular to the organism to which the cell belonged. In the words of Frederick Copleston, 'Driesch became convinced that in the organic body there was an autonomous active principle which directs the vital processes and which cannot be accounted for by a purely mechanistic theory of life'.[8] Although Hönigswald did not necessarily accept Driesch's theory of vitalism, he was grateful that Driesch seemed to have shown scientifically that reality could not be satisfactorily explained by mechanistic theories alone. This enabled Hönigswald to take the step described by Grassl as 'from medicine to methodology'.[9]

The methodology that Hönigswald ultimately arrived at was given by him the name 'Denkpsychologie', a term that is difficult to translate. Literally it can be rendered as 'thought or thinking psychology'; but the term 'psychology' is misleading

[7] R. Grassl, *Der junge Richard Hönigswald. Eine biographisch fundierte Kontextualisierung in historischer Absicht* (Studien und Materialen zum Neu-kantianismus 13), Würzburg: Königshausen & Neumann, 1998.
[8] F. Copleston, *A History of Philosophy, vol. 7, Modern Philosophy Part II Schopenhauer to Nietzsche*, New York: Image Books, 1965, Part 2, p.157.
[9] Grassl, *Junge Hönigswald*, p.132.

in both German and English if it suggests a link with either humanistic or experimental psychology. As understood by Hönigswald, 'Denkpsychologie' was essentially an epistemological discipline, that is, one concerned to examine critically the structures and limitations of perception.[10]

An attempt will now be made to sketch Hönigswald's path to Denkpsychologie, in order to clarify the exact parameters of his thought. This is a very complicated matter, involving the central issues of nineteenth- and twentieth-century German philosophy, and a brief outline will almost certainly be superficial and in some respects possibly misleading.

Immanuel Kant, in his critical philosophy, had tried to answer the question 'What can I know?' by examining the conditions and structures of the possibility of perceiving objects. This raised the question of the 'Ding an sich', 'Thing-in-itself'.[11] Did the things that were perceived exist independently of being perceived by subjects (persons)? Kant's answer was that if they did, nothing could be known about them; nevertheless, they needed to be postulated (presumed). Similar questions arose about laws of nature, logic, mathematics and concepts such as time, space and number. Some of Kant's followers were less critical than he, and speculated about realms of existence beyond human perception. As a reaction, there arose a 'back to Kant movement', usually called Neo-Kantianism, but there were many variations within this movement. In some quarters attempts were made to get rid of the idea of the thing-in-itself idea altogether.[12]

[10] See further J. Kosian, 'Richard Hönigswalds Denkpsychologie' in E.O. Orth, D. Aleksandrowicz (eds.), *Studien zur Philosophie Richard Hönigswalds* (Studien und Materialen zum Neukantianismus 7), Würzburg: Königshausen & Neumann, 1996, pp.37-48.
[11] Beiser (see footnote 12) consistently has 'Thing-in-itself.
[12] F. C. Beiser, *The Fate of Reason. German Philosophy from Kant to Fichte*, Cambridge, Mass.: Harvard University Press, 1987, pp.307-9. Hönigswald,

Hönigswald's *Denkpsychologie* was a critical examination of the way in which objects were perceived by subjects (persons). Because each perceiving person was a unique individual, each object which was perceived was perceived and understood in a unique way. The moment of perception was a unique encounter between a perceiving 'I' and a *Gegenstand* (object), a German word which has the sense of something standing (the *stand* element of the term) over against (German *Gegen*) the perceiving 'I'. Objects were 'I' determined. Underlying this position was Hönigswald's use of the concept of the 'monad' which he took from Leibniz. The monad as described by the Leibniz expert Hans Heinz Holz was not something made up of various elements, although it was that, but 'the creation of of a higher unity in which the parts give up their particular independence in order to build an individual whole'.[13]

It is easy to see how this appealed to Hönigswald, the former medical student in a faculty where human beings were studied and treated from a purely physical/chemical and causal/mechanical viewpoint. According to Leibniz's idea of the monad, the physical/chemical elements that made up a human being lost their particularity as they combined together to produce something individual and unique. The same was true in perception. In the moment that the 'I' perceived an object, a coalescence of elements came about whose combination was unique. The purpose of Hönigswald's *Denkpsychologie* was to examine critically the implications of this view for theories of knowledge and of science.

---

following his teacher Alois Riehl, saw the value of the notion of the Thing-In-Itself, but developed it in a distinctive way. See R. Breil, *Hönigswald und Kant*, Bonn: Bouvier Verlag, 1991, p.23.

[13] H.H. Holz, ed. by J. Zimmer *Leibniz. Das Lebenswerk eines Universalgelehrten*, Darmstadt: WB, 2013, p.46. 'Die Herstellung einer höheren Einheit, in der die Teile ihre vereinzelte Selbständigkeit aufgeben, um ein individuelles Ganzes zu bilden.'

One of the outcomes of this approach was that Hönigswald argued that each academic discipline was unique. This was in stark contrast to the Marburg School of Neo-Kantians that regarded mathematics as the academic discipline to which all other disciplines should be reduced. But biology was not, according to Hönigswald, to be treated in the same way as physics, nor in the same way as chemistry or mathematics. Further, the humanities, including ethics, history, art and religion, all had their special 'monadic' (in a broad sense) nature. The task of scholarship, whatever else it involved, was ultimately to investigate and understand the monads, not to explain them away or dissolve them into their constituent elements. The task of philosophy was to examine critically the epistemological nature of the separate and appropriate study of each aspect of the natural and human world.

This philosophical, critical examination was carried out by a rigorous logical examination of the language used in each discipline. For Hönigswald, inter-subjectivity, that is, the common element that enabled monads to interact, was language; and language used or contained concepts (German *Begriffe*) that could be logically investigated in order to arrive at meanings that monads had in common. A regular feature of Hönigswald's argumentation is the phrase '*Es gehört zum Begriff...*' 'It pertains (or belongs) to the concept of...' and the same is frequently found in Lohmeyer.

A consequence of this was that it was possible to reach conclusions about inter-subjective meanings that would not necessarily be apparent to the language users themselves. A parallel would be the grammatical or linguistic descriptions of language use which are not apparent to speakers or users of languages. This also meant that it was possible to interrogate the language use of ancient texts and to discuss concepts of which the ancient writers/speakers would have been unaware. This will be demonstrated later in this chapter when Hönigswald's essay on the Genesis creation narrative is considered in detail. For the moment, it can be noted that a criticism brought against Lohmeyer, that his account of the thought of Paul would not have been apparent to Paul himself, failed to understand the method that Lohmeyer was applying to Pauline texts.

Hönigswald's understanding of history emphasised the importance of the subjective element and of the 'the now-ness' of the experience of time. The point at which we experience the past and the present is *now*, and each monad experiences it uniquely. But what is today called 'cultural memory' is an important element in a monad's present experience of the past. Indeed, the term 'cultural memory' introduces the concept of culture, an element in Hönigswald's thinking that cannot be further examined here. What is important for present purposes is the emphasis found in both Hönigswald and Lohmeyer that each event in history is not only unique, but universal, in the sense that within its dynamics is the clue to or meaning of all 'history'. Lohmeyer is fond of quoting from Leopold von Ranke and from Goethe in this regard (see below, p.125).

Sufficient has been said by way of introduction to Hönigswald's thought. The remainder of this chapter will concern itself with Hönigswald's discussion of the account of creation in the book of Genesis. It is a representative example of his philosophical method and has the added advantage of dealing with a biblical matter.

Hönigswald published his essay *Erkenntnistheoretisches zur Schöpfungsgeschichte der Genesis (Epistemological Questions*

Regarding the Account of Creation in Genesis) in 1932,[14] long after his formative contact with Lohmeyer in Breslau. However, as he wrote in the preface, the publication was the fruit of many years of reflecting and teaching on the subject, so that we can safely assume that its general approach would not have been unfamiliar to Lohmeyer.

Hönigswald begins by stating emphatically that he is not attempting a history of religions approach, one that compares the Genesis creation account with ones from the Ancient World that might have influenced it. He is concerned only with epistemology, that is, with the philosophical assumptions of the concepts, such as of origin, world, world origin, that are found in the creation stories. Such concepts have philosophical presuppositions, even if these were not apparent to the writers of the creation narratives, which can be elucidated and examined contextually (p.6).

All creation accounts (cosmogonies) are concerned with the *substance*, with the coming into being of *something*, by means of *events*, that make up a *world* of a particular kind. That particularity is not arbitrary, but has an intrinsic value, which can be traced to a Creator. Because events are involved, the notion of *causality* is implicit, as is the notion of *order*. There are, however, cosmogonies that speak of the existence of chaos. Hönigswald argues that chaos and created order are only relative notions, the main difference being that chaos cannot be understood as a 'whole', whereas created order can be thus understood. Again, created order implies activity on the part of a Creator, who acts (*handelt*).

---

[14] R. Hönigswald, *Erkenntnistheoretisches zur Schöpfungsgeschichte der Genesis*, Sammlung Gemeinverständliche Vorträge und Schriften aus dem Gebiet der Theologie und Religionsgeschichte 161, Tübingen: J. C. B. Mohr, 1932.

A particular question that troubles Hönigswald at this point is that writers of cosmogonies describe the origin of worlds that are not directly concerned with ourselves; yet we are part of their world and, paradoxically, we can only explain their origin from *within*, from a viewpoint that does not allow us to see worlds as a whole. Yet it pertains to the nature of a created order to have an ordered wholeness (pp.9-10).

The matter of the personification of forces of nature leads, in Hönigswald's discussion, to an outline of the ways in which cosmogonies speak of subordinate gods and forces, some of which make chaos less chaotic by having functions within chaos, others of which appear in nature as superstitious forces which may need to be appeased by sacrifices and rituals. An important question is how the created order is *sustained* after it has been brought into existence. Hönigswald sees an element of pantheism in cosmogonies as an explanation of how the created order is sustained. Also, dialectical tensions can be found, for example, in Iranian and Indian cosmogonies, between good and bad principles, and being and non-being as 'forces' that are imminent in existence.

Another factor is that of naming. Hönigswald cites the opening of the Babylonian creation epic (without explicitly naming *Enûma Eliš*): 'When heaven above was not yet named and earth beneath no names did carry ... when the gods were not yet created or named ...' (p.16) to stress the importance of naming in the process of making the created order intelligible and giving it ethical values and ultimate aims (*Weltzwecke)*. Suddenly, he now turns to the Genesis narrative which, he maintains, is quite different from the other cosmogonies from the epistemological-theoretical viewpoint. It is childlike (*kindlich*) and naïve, yet of the greatest significance (p.17).

Hönigswald is fully aware of the results of the critical study of the Old Testament and the Genesis creation story. The implicit monotheism of the story is the result of a development from polytheism, and its God, Jahwe, is a West Semitic deity who becomes increasingly bound up with Israel's history, and disconnected from nature. However, whatever its origins might have been, the biblical account of creation, as we have it, can be seen as a unity with a clear and distinctive epistemological-theological character, which can be described as 'biblical monotheism' (p.18). This phrase is crucial. It is not that the notion of monotheism can be applied to the biblical Creator God. On the contrary, the functions that are attributed to the biblical Creator *define the nature of Israelite monotheism* (p.18).

God, in the Genesis account, is not distinct from any kind of chaos. The chaos is part of his work; neither are there any intermediaries between God and the creative act. Hönigswald deals with the divine Word later in the essay and does not see it as an intermediate factor. The creation is an *action* (*Tathandlung*). This action is complete in itself; God is no 'first cause', the factor that begins a chain of events. But to form an action is to have an intention, and to act freely to achieve it. In the case of Genesis the intention is a moral one (*sittlich*) and opens the way to a view of the Creator in personal terms, one that also opens the way to personal prayer (*den Weg des persönlichen Gebetes*, p.21). Yet the text is not speaking of the *personification* of some aspect of the world. God's creative action is an absolute act of freedom.

A good deal of space is devoted to the notion of 'beginning' (*Anfang*) in the various parts of the essay. 'Beginning' is, after all, the very first word of the Genesis account, and although Hönigswald does not make anything of this, he is insistent that in Genesis, 'beginning' cannot have the sense of the first point in a sequence. The biblical idea of 'beginning' is that of the timelessness of the completeness of what God has done (p.22). Hönigswald refers to the understanding of time on the part of the mystics, especially Meister Eckhart. Everything in God is a 'now', a 'beginning', without becoming. The moment in which God speaks is also the 'now' of the last day (p.23). While other cosmogonies speak of a beginning in a temporal sense, this is not so in Genesis; and if 'beginning' in Genesis has an historical sense, its meaning is that the unfolding history of the world has an intended plan, '[eine] Fortgesetzt wirksames Planhaftigheit' (p.24).

Returning to the mention of the Creator as personal (not as a person), Hönigswald introduces one of his central epistemological ideas, that of the monad, and the way in which the monad experiences objects (*Gegenstände*), so that a unique relationship ensues which changes both the monad and the object experienced. But the monad is not an isolated individual, but 'part of a community of appropriately interacting monads' *(eine verständigungsgemäßen Gemeinschaft der Monaden*, p.26). Hönigswald argues that this state of affairs is grounded ultimately in a *monas monadum* (a monas of monads) that embraces the sense (*Sinn*) of each inter-monadic community. Whether or not this amounts to a proof of God's existence, Hönigswald insists that this stress on personal interaction takes the matter into the dimension of mutual understanding, revelation and confession.

The argument now reverts to the notion of 'beginning'. Granted that the God of the Genesis creation story is the Israelite national God, this 'limitation' is seen by Hönigswald to offer possibilities of the greatest possible expansion (*größtmögliche Erweiterung*, p.27). The biblical idea of 'beginnning', viewed critically, implies the believing community of all people, and it is in that sense that Christianity follows on from Judaism, not in the sense of an historical development, but logically from the biblical notion of 'beginning'. Jewish belief in a God-given Messiah is a way of uniting past and future in a new form of blessed present.

Hönigswald now deals with the 'Word' which features prominently in the Genesis account. Whereas, in the Babylonian account, naming is important and also implies the fate of things, the biblical account is quite different. The naming that occurs in Genesis 1 is not categorical, that is, it does not assign things to particular categories by naming them. The naming is signative (*signativ*), that is, it signifies or identifies that which already exists within their categories. The Word is a function of the notion of 'beginning'. But the Word is also tied to the monad and to its implicit intersubjective communication and community, in that it is speech that makes such intersubjectivity possible. Further, since the Creator is the Monad of monads, it belongs to his being that he must communicate with other monads, and thus he cannot create *silently*. It also follows that the Creator is a *Thou* (*du*), who speaks and reveals.

At the end of the essay Hönigswald cites the prologue to John's Gospel as that which truly reflects the epistemological structure of the Genesis creation account: 'In the beginning was the Word.' This implies that there was meaning and that meaning was an action. 'In the beginning was the deed (action), for only the deed is the beginning'.[15]

---

[15] This is an allusion to Goethe's *Faust*, edited A E Schöne, Frankfurt: Deutsche Klassiker Verlag, 1994, p.61, Act I, lines 1224-1233.

Hönigswald's treatment of the Genesis creation account is not an exercise in biblical interpretation. It makes no attempt to read the text in the context of the Old Testament as a whole. This is most obvious in the treatment of the function of the 'Word' in Genesis, and the many links that can be made with passages in the Psalms (e.g., Psalm 33.6: 'By the word of the Lord were the heavens made') and the prophets (e.g., Jeremiah 1.4: 'The Word of the Lord came to me'). All these are ignored. What we have instead is an exposition of the Creation narrative, in which the text is treated as something whose key terms can be subjected to a critical analysis, underpinned by Hönigswald's *Denkpsychologie*. Sometimes the logical leaps are very large, and not always convincing, especially in the discussion of the term 'beginning'; and readers can be forgiven for not always following the argument as I have tried to summarise it.

In support of Hönigswald it can be said that biblical scholars have not usually thought about the philosophical implications of concepts such as 'time' and 'beginning'. There has also been a tendency to try to conform the opening words of Genesis to what is found in the Babylonian creation epic, as in the New English Bible rendering, 'In the beginning of creation, when God made heaven and earth …'. There is an unexamined philosophical assumption in this rendering, which puts it clearly at odds with Hönigswald's interpretation. Another striking point is Hönigswald's statement that it is the biblical text which should determine what biblical monotheism is. Biblical scholars mostly apply an unexamined concept of monotheism to the Bible, an unexamined concept in which hide theories about the evolution of something called 'religion', another term that is used in an unexamined way.

However, the present book is not about Hönigswald but about Lohmeyer! The value of the essay on the Genesis creation narrative for the purposes of this book lies in the fact that Lohmeyer advocates Hönigswald's *Denkpsychologie* and often applies his methods of concept analysis to key terms in the biblical text. This will become clearer in later chapters, and will be pointed out where necessary. There is one respect in which Lohmeyer's approach differed from that of Hönigswald. Hönigswald's treatment of Genesis 1 makes no reference to the literary structure of the passage; to the fact that creation, including God's resting at the end takes seven days, of which the fourth day is pivotal. Such matters were of great importance for Lohmeyer, as will be demonstrated, and part of that importance came from Lohmeyer's interest in the poetic work of Stefan George, the subject of the next chapter.

Friedrich Gundolf

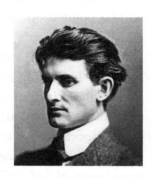

Richard Hönigswald

Stefan George

CHAPTER TWO

Stefan George

The poet Stefan Anton George was born on 12 July 1868 in a village close to Bingen, in the wine-growing area where the River Nahe joins the Rhine. George's father worked in the wine trade. In 1873 the family moved to Bingen itself. From 1882-88 George studied at the grammar school (*Gymnasium*) in Darmstadt, from which time his earliest poems are dated. In 1888, on completing his *Abitur* (university entrance requirement), he travelled to London and Switzerland, followed by journeys to Italy, Paris, Spain and Berlin; and from 1889-91 George studied in the Philosophical Faculty in Berlin.

George never had a permanent place in which he lived.[16] He retained a room in his parents' house in Bingen, but preferred to travel all over Europe and to stay for short, extended periods in Berlin with the artist and painter Reinhold Lepsius, in Munich with Karl Wolfskehl, and in Heidelberg with Friedrich Gundolf. At the end of his life he spent more and more time in the Swiss Canton of Ticino, and for his final illness in a nursing home in Locarno, where he died in December 1933. For present purposes the most important connection was that with Heidelberg, where Gundolf was a professor of literature. Lohmeyer's wife was one of Gundolf's students, and Lohmeyer himself taught briefly in Heidelberg from the end of 1918-20.

---

[16] F. Schönauer, *Stefan George in Selbstzeugnissen und Bilddokumenten.* Reinbek-bei-Hamburg: Rowohlt Verlag, 1969, p.59.

Edgar Salin, who was a student in Heidelberg shortly before the outbreak of the First World War, has left a vivid description of George at that time, and of his impact upon those who belonged to his circle.[17] George had an imposing physical presence, with a very high forehead topped by a mass of hair,[18] although he was only of middle height.[19] In his conversation, especially with his younger followers, he had an irresistible humanity, although at the same time he could make people feel foolish if they did not understand him. His closest followers either feared his words of disapproval, for example, of the way they read aloud, or they were elated to receive praise from him. They stood in awe of him.

Gundolf's book on George,[20] itself a work of art in its own right, sees George standing in the succession to Goethe and Hölderlin as a poetic seer able to describe the future in the poetic now. For George, poetry was to be pure art for its own sake and certainly not to be a vehicle for national, political or social aims; and yet, especially against the industrialisation and war of the first part of the twentieth century, poetry was to envision a new Germany, a Germany of a poetical, spiritual nature, whose standard-bearers were to be the young men who belonged to his circle. It was that vision of a new and spiritual nation that attracted young men such as the Stauffenberg brothers, and inspired their resistance to National Socialism. The National Socialists themselves (Joseph Goebbels had been a student of Gundolf) would have liked to use George for their own purposes, but his absence from Germany during his final years and his death in 1933 prevented them from doing so.

---

[17] E. Salin, *Um Stefan George*. Godesberg: Verlag Helmut Küpper, 1948.
[18] *See* Schönauer for many photographs and paintings.
[19] Salin, p.26
[20] F. Gundolf: *George*, Berlin: Georg Bondi, 1930, 3rd edition of the 1920 book.

George's poetic works were published, from the end of the nineteenth century, by Georg Bondi. The books were artistic in themselves, printed on thick paper with a distinctive Roman typeface, which reproduced George's eccentric refusal to use capital letters for nouns. Also reproduced were examples of George's handwritten poems in his distinctive, not-joined-up style of writing for poems.

The remainder of this chapter will outline George's collection of poems entitled *The Seventh Ring*, which appeared in 1907. It is an illuminating example of George's art and thought, but also of interest because Lohmeyer made much of the importance of the number seven in his commentary on the Book of Revelation.[21] Of course, Lohmeyer did not read the number seven into Revelation; and, as he pointed out, this number could also be found in other Jewish apocalypses.[22] But Lohmeyer made much more of this fact than had been the case with commentaries on Revelation before or since, and it is likely that he was not unaffected by George's use of the number seven in his structure of *The Seventh Ring*.

The central part of this collection is entitled 'Maximin'. George had first met Maximilian Kronberger in Munich early in 1902, when the youth was aged 14.[23] Initial acquaintance led to Kronberger being taken into the George circle, a relationship that was tragically ended by Kronberger's death from meningitis in April 1904, the day after his sixteenth birthday.

Gundolf is at pains to point out that George's interest in Kronberger was not sexual erotic, but platonic.[24] It was

---

[21] E. Lohmeyer, *Die Offenbarung des Johannes* (Handbuch zum Neuen Testament 16), Tübingen: J. C. B. Mohr (Paul Siebeck), 1926.
[22] Lohmeyer, *Offenbarung*, p.182
[23] Schönauer, p.103
[24] Gundolf, p.202

George's calling, as a poet-prophet, to reveal in his poetry the divine as he found it in young German manhood at its strongest and purist. Maximilian Kronberger seems to have revealed what George had been searching for, a fact made tragic by the young man's death. The first of the poems in the section 'Maximin', entitled 'Advent I', reads as follows:

> To some you are a child,
> To some a friend, to me
> The god whom I divined
> And tremble to adore,
> You came at last when sick
> With waiting, weary of
> My prayers I began
> To lose myself in night.
>
> I knew you by the beam
> Which flowed into my dark,
> The step to which the seer
> Replied with sudden bloom.[25]

However, the opening section contains fourteen (twice seven) 'Poems of Our Times', each one with four verses of eight lines. The final poem, 'A Poem of My Times', begins:

> I am your conscience, I the voice pervading,
> Your malcontent that curses and condemns:
> You turned away from grandeur and from beauty
> Because it was your purpose to deny them ...
> Like seekers after gold who, pale and fevered,
> Were bowed on crucibles with ore and fluxes
> While sunlight paths unrolled beneath their windows,
> So you concocted souls from filth and poison
> And spilled the residue of healthy saps.

---

[25] O. Marx and E. Morwitz (trans.), *The Works of Stefan George. Rendered into English*, Chapel Hill: University of North Carolina Press, 2nd edition, 1974, p.257. German: *Der siebente Ring*, Berlin: Georg Bondi, 1914, p.96.

Against this denial of beauty which had led to so much that is base and tawdry in human life, George articulated his vision, expressing a truth known from the time of the Pharaohs:

> That deserts shift with gardens, frost with blaze,
> Night comes for sin, atonement for delight.
> And though despair and dark engulf us, one thing
> There always was (none knows it) is eternal,
> And youth and flowers laugh and songs resound.[26]

Gundolf makes it clear in a remarkable passage that George's strictures against what has been blind and unseeing in the human rejection of beauty, and the consequent deforming of human life that has ensued, are not the strictures of disillusionment, but the inevitable consequence of a positive 'Yes', deriving from a vision of hope:

> The negative judgements of Hölderlin and Nietzsche are misunderstood when they are taken to be the complaints of malcontent. All curses and denials of prophets take their meaning from an unconditional 'Yes' demanded by the appearance of a new god. Without meaning to, each 'Yes' entails a 'No', each eternity necessarily creates mere time; every beginning an end; every space, limits; every height a depth. But it is the prophets, those who proclaim new gods, i.e., people of the turning point (*Wende*) whose 'Yes' is at the same time reproof and judgement, and appears to a self-satisfied generation to be no more than deniers so long as their new god, their new 'Yes', is not recognised.[27]

---

[26] Marx and Morwitz, p.229, German p.33.

[27] Gundolf, p.221, 'Man mißversteht sie ebenso wie die Gedichte Hölderlins und Nietzsches, wenn man sie als die Anklagen eines Mißvergnügten nimmt. Erst, von dem unbedingten Ja aus, von dem Erscheinen eines neuen Gottes, der fordert, haben alle Flüche und Verneinungen der Propheten ihren Sinn. Ganz unwillkürlich setzt jedes neue Ja sein Nein, ganz unausweichlich schafft jede Ewigkeit eine bloße Zeit, jeder Beginn ein Ende, jeder Raum Grenzen und jede Höhe eine Tiefe. Aber es sind die Profeten, die Künder neuer Götter, also Menschen der Wende, deren Ja zugleich Rüge und Gericht wird, und die einem ganzen selbstgefälligen Zeitalter als Verneiner vorkommen, solange man ihren neuen Gott, ihr neues Ja noch nicht wahrnimmt'.

Gundolf's view of George as a prophet can be seen clearly in these words. Through his poetry, George has brought to expression his vision of the divine as revealed in what is most beautifully human. His vision, expressed in his poetry, inevitably shows a world that is ugly and deformed in so far as it cannot recognise the divine as the prophet sees it.

Clemens Heselhaus regards the 'Poems of Our Time' as the most important part of *The Seventh Ring*, and subjects them to a detailed rhythmic analysis.[28] He argues that the impact of the poems depends not only on the images evoked by the choice of words, but on the use of rhythm, and the need to raise and lower the voice. Salin[29] has vividly described how important it was, when a passage was being read to George, to get the accent and the rhythm to George's satisfaction, and how searing his criticism could be when such reading did not meet his demands. Heselhaus gives as an example the way in which significant and important words are juxtaposed in the poem, 'A Poem of My Times'. It can also be noted that against George's custom of not using capital letters for nouns, two nouns, *Körper* (body) and *Boden* (soil) do have capital letters:

> Ihr hobet über Körper weg und Boden
> Aus rauch und staub und dunst den bau | schon wuchsen
> In riesenformen mauern bogen türme ...

> Beyond the body and the soil, you lifted
> Your house of smoke, and dust, and fog. The spires,
> The walls, and arches rose and grew gigantic.[30]

He also notes how the number seven binds together what is otherwise not a very unified collection. There are fourteen

---

[28] C. Heselhaus, *Deutsche Lyrik der Moderne von Nietzsche bis Yvan Goll*, Düsseldorf: August Bagel Verlag, 1961, pp.95-114.

[29] Salin, pp.24-25

[30] O. Marx and E. Morwitz (trans.), *The Works of Stefan George*, p.229. German: *Der siebente Ring*, p.32.

'Time' poems, fourteen 'Pageant' poems, twenty headed 'Tides', twenty-one about Maximin, fourteen headed 'Darkness of Dream', twenty-eight 'Songs' and seventeen 'Tablets'.[31] Among the 'Pageant' poems is one entitled 'The Anti-Christ'. It is a remarkable assemblage of allusions to the Bible, which present a picture of a worker of wonders and inspirer of false hopes, all of which are based upon a cynical aim to deceive and lead into disaster, while victims are left to flounder without help or hope:

> The sky has no marvels I cannot confer,
> A hairsbreadth amiss, but you do not discern
> The hoax, for your senses are blunted.[32]

In a passage that Lohmeyer must surely have known, Gundolf described this poem in terms linked to the Book of Revelation:

> 'The Antichrist' is the gigantic final form of a secularised national life that perverts every truth, soothes every anxiety and sucks the blood from every reason. The falsifier, the dazzler, the ensnarer, the mis-user, the confuser, the 'prince of vermin', who makes what is difficult, pleasant and cheap for everyone; who corrupts what exists, perverts the arts, bends the standards, falsifies what is true – the demon of corruption, the herald of disaster, hedged between flabby nature and lustful spirit. The abolition of Christianity, the degenerate spirit and world of souls has found here a mighty unveiling (*Apokalypse*), as in the vision from Patmos of the fall of the heathen world of blood and sensuality. This poem alone would put George in the ranks of the great prophets. It has nothing to compare with it for its visionary flight, its dark greatness, its plastic energy and thundering distance.[33]

---

[31] Heselhaus, p.106

[32] Marks and Morwitz, p.240, German p.56.

[33] '"Der Widerchrist" ist die gigantische Endgestalt des entgotteten Völkerlebens, die jede Wahrheit umkehrt, jedes Gesetz umgeht, jeden Quell trübt und jeden Grund aussaugt ... der Fälscher, der Blender, der Umgarner, der Mißbraucher, der Wirrer, "der Fürst des Geziefers", der das Schwere bequem und billig-massenhaft macht, das Wesen nach-scheint, die Künste vor-täuscht,

The third main section of *The Seventh Ring* consists of 70 *Tafeln* ('Tablets'). Most consist of four lines of poetry, and whereas the 'Time' poems avoided rhyme, the 'Tablets' are replete with rhymes, sometimes with rhyming couplets, sometimes with the final and third and second and fourth lines rhyming. Some of the 'Tablets' are addressed to members of George's circle, such as Karl and Hanna Wolfskehl, Gundolf, and Albert Verwey. According to Gundolf, the final section of *The Seventh Ring* addresses its topics in the light of the discovery of the divine, especially as articulated in the 'Maximin' section. The 'Tablets' are prophetic in the narrow sense of the word: they are 'seherrische Vorwegnahme der Zukunft in der Zeit' ('visionary anticipations of the future in the [present] time').[34]

In another remarkable passage, Gundolf claims that:

> Nations are first created by gods ... this has been known by every seer from biblical times to Hölderlin, and has named the god together with the nation ... Such a seer ... feels the coming fate of the nation most intensely, for in the new god everything is there that he brings and demands. Being a seer is only the present receiving of his outpouring light which only reaches the darker distant places later ... It is less a seeing in advance of what will happen in the future and more an immediate discerning of what is already on its way.[35]

---

das Grade biegt das Ächte ersetzt – der Dämon des Schwindels, der Vorbote des Untergangs, geheckt zwischen der schlaffen Natur und dem geilen Geist. Die Endschaft der Christenheit, die entartete Geist- und Seelenwelt hat hier eine gleich gewaltige Apokalypse gefunden wie im Gesicht von Patmos der Verfall der heidnischen Blut- und Sinnenwelt. Dies Gedicht allein würde George schon in die Reihe der großen Propheten stellen: es hat kaum seinesgleichen an visionärem Flug, düsterer Großheit, plastischer Wucht und donnernder Ferne. Gundolf, p.232.

[34] Gundolf, p.241.

[35] Gundolf, p.242. 'Erst durch Götter werden Völker geschaffen ... das hat von den biblischcen Zeiten bis zu Hölderlin jeder Seher gewußt, und den Gott mit dem Volk zusammen aufgerufen. Ein solcher fühlt auch am eignen Leib ... am unmittelbarsten die kommenden Geschicke des Volkes ... denn im neuen Gott ist alles schon da was er bringt und fordert. Sehertum ist nur der gegenwärtige

Lohmeyer's commentary on the Book of Revelation will be dealt with in a later chapter. Its use of the number seven has already been mentioned, but what is striking about the commentary is its concluding pages which address general matters concerning the biblical book. To read this section, having read Gundolf on George, is to feel that one is breathing the same air; that the section could almost have been written by Gundolf himself. Lohmeyer notes that whereas Jewish apocalypses often use a figure drawn from antiquity (e.g., Enoch, Daniel) to be the recipient of visions of the future, so that past and future are bound together, the seer (Lohmeyer frequently uses the word *'Seher'*) in Revelation lives in the present and that the last times are bound up with the present. The seer is a poet and a prophet, whose faith-filled present (*glaubenserfüllte Gegenwart*) is bound up with the eschatological future.[36] There will be more to say about this later. For the moment, it is sufficient to note that Lohmeyer thought and wrote like no-one else in the New Testament scholarship of his day (or since), and that some of his originality makes better sense if seen in the light of George and Gundolf.

Empfang seiner Strahlung, welche die Dumpferen Ferneren erst später erreicht ... weniger ein Vorhersehen dessen was eintreffen wird als ein Zuerst-spüren dessen was da oder unterwegs ist'.
[36] Lohmeyer, *Offenbarung*, p.196.

CHAPTER THREE

Diatheke (Covenant)

Lohmeyer's *Diatheke. Ein Beitrag zur Erklärung des neu-testamentlichen Begriffs* was published in 1913.[37] It was the published version of the doctoral dissertation that he defended in Berlin in July 1912. The foreword to the book was written in Schloß Gaffron bei Raudten (today, Rudna, 43 miles north-west of Wrocław), where Lohmeyer was working as a private tutor.[38] Its importance for the present book lies in the fact that it bears no trace of the influence of Hönigswald or the George circle. It deals with a *Begriff* (term), namely, the Greek word *diathēkē*, but the treatment is at the level of determining its meaning in the context of its usage in the world of biblical antiquity. It is quite different from the way in which Lohmeyer would later treat *Begriffe in* a manner derived from Hönigswald, in which a 'term' or 'concept' (*Begriff*) was assumed to have a kind of universal logical structure, which could be investigated by means of Denkpsychologie. The book *Diatheke* indicates what kind of scholar Lohmeyer would have been had he not become interested in Hönigswald's philosophy and the literary theories of the George circle; and it must be said at once that *Diatheke* shows that he would have become an outstanding representative of conventional German New Testament scholarship. That he chose to follow a different path from that of his contemporaries led eventually

---

[37] Ernst Lohmeyer, *Diatheke. Ein Beitrag zur Erklärung des neutestamentlichen Begriffs* (*Untersuchungen zum Neuen Testament*), Hans Windisch (ed.), Leipzig: J. C. Heinrichs'sche Buchhandlung, 1913.
[38] Köhn, p.8

to his becoming marginalised and forgotten. This was a tragedy, because what he had to offer in his eccentricity was far too valuable to be ignored.

By any standards, Lohmeyer's doctoral dissertation was a work of outstanding scholarship. It displayed an encyclopaedic coverage of Classical sources, papyri, inscriptions, Jewish Rabbinic texts, and Jewish Apocrypha and Pseudepigrapha. Especially interesting for a modern reader is the fact that Lohmeyer discussed the so-called 'Damascus Document' that today is connected with the so-called 'Dead Sea Scrolls', discovered after 1947. The Damascus Document, discovered in the Cairo Geniza, had been published in 1910 by Solomon Schechter.

The central question that Lohmeyer addressed was whether the term *'Diatheke'* in the New Testament was to be understood as Luther had appeared to have understood it, as a testament, or as a covenant. The basic difference was that a testament was a one-way bestowal of property or status (such as adoption), while a covenant was an agreement between two parties, each with mutual obligations. The whole issue has been more recently addressed by Ernst Kutsch.[39] The first chapter dealt with Ancient Greek usage in papyri, inscriptions and literary sources, as well as Jewish texts, and indicated that the main sense of *Diatheke* was that of a testament in the sense of a Last Will and Testament. However, Lohmeyer admitted that this sense was not as sharp as in current legal understanding, and that it could contain elements of mutual obligation.[40]

---

[39] E. Kutsch, *Neues Testament – Neuer Bund? Eine Fehlübersetzung wird korrigiert.* Neukirchen-Vluyn: Neukirchener Verlag, 1978.
[40] In novels of our own time, of course, if not in reality, a Last Will and Testament can lay obligations on a recipient.

Chapter 2 is entitled 'Berith im Alten Testament'. It has to be read, of course, in the light of the state of Old Testament criticism that existed at the beginning of the twentieth century. This confidently dated the non-priestly narratives of the Pentateuch and the books from Joshua to II Kings to the Pre-Exilic period, Deuteronomy to the seventh century, and Jeremiah, Ezekiel and Isaiah 40-55 to the period immediately prior to and during the Exile in the sixth century. It also traced a religious development from the Pre-Exilic period, through the eighth-century prophets, to Deuteronomy. Given this state of scholarship, Lohmeyer's treatment was thorough and impressive.

He divided the chapter into two main parts: profane senses of the Hebrew term *berith*, which he saw as occurring primarily in the Pre-Exilic period and their sources; and a religious sense of *berith*, which he saw as developing out of and away from the profane sense. In the Pre-Exilic, profane, uses of *berith*, as found in narratives such as Genesis 31.43-54 (the covenant between Laban and Jacob) or I Samuel 18.1-4 (the covenant between David and Jonathan), a *berith* was certainly an arrangement in which both sides had obligations. Lohmeyer summed up the use of *berith* in its profane sense as follows:

> According to its character and the relation of the parties to each other, [the word *berith*] takes on the meanings of covenant, treaty, promise, obligation or vow. 'Berith' is a vessel which can be filled with the most varied contents. What remains constant is the character of irrevocability and permanance which it gives to these terms.[41]

---

[41] 'Je nach dem Charakter dieser und der Stellung der beiden Parteien zueinander erhält sie die bestimmtere Bedeutung vom Bund, Vertrag, Zusicherung, Verpflichtung, Gulübde. So ist Berith wie ein Gefäß, in das sich die verschiedensten Inhalte füllen lassen. Diese werden nur zusammengefaßt durch den Charakter der Unlösbarkeit und Stetigkeit, den sie ihnen gibt'. *Diatheke*, p.45.

The section on the religious sense of *berith* is divided into several sub-sections: a) The time of the first 'writing prophets'; b) the time of the great prophets (Amos, Hosea, First Isaiah), Deuteronomy, Jeremiah, Ezekiel, Second Isaiah; c) Early Judaism. The first section deals mainly with the Sinai Covenant, whose historicity Lohmeyer defends by saying that its importance for the prophetic books and Chronicles would be impossible had it not actually occurred. The Sinai Covenant involved mutual obligations on the part of the people and Yahveh, which could be summed up in the formula, 'Yahveh, the God of Israel; Israel, the people of Yahveh'.[42] It was not a 'natural' relationship that was thus formed, but resulted from God's free grace towards his people.

To the objection that if the Sinai Covenant was so important it is strange that it was so seldom later mentioned, Lohmeyer replied that the relationship between Yahveh and Israel was so much the reality in which the faith of the nation was lived, that it was not necessary for the tradition to keep mentioning the origins or causes of the relationship. This was perhaps the weakest part of Lohmeyer's argument, because he had earlier defended the historicity of the Sinai Covenant traditions on account of their importance for later writers. Lohmeyer elegantly skirted around the thorny problems of whether the Decalogue was a fundamental part of the Sinai Covenant, which part Moses had to play in it, and what the significance of the Ark of the Covenant was.[43] He doubted whether there had been a covenant with the tribe of Levi (compare Deuteronomy 10.8-9), but a covenant with the House of David was certain, although no account of its enactment was extant.[44]

---

[42] p.53
[43] p.55, note 4
[44] Lohmeyer relied on II Samuel 23.1-7, which he held to be the basis for II Samuel 7, not vice versa. See p.56, note 5.

In the section on Amos, Lohmeyer noted that although the term *berith* did not occur in the book in the religious sense, it was implied in the words of Amos 3:2, 'You only have I known of all the families of the earth', with the people's obligations expressed in the following clause, 'Therefore I will punish you for your iniquities.' Hosea was a different case. The word *berith* occurred in a religious sense twice, at 6:7 ('At Adam they transgressed the covenant') and 8:1 ('They have broken my covenant'). Both passages implied a covenant of mutual obligation. A new element in Hosea was the use of the idea of marriage to describe Yahveh's relationship with his people. Lohmeyer based himself on Hosea 1:1-3, which he believed mirrored the prophet's personal experience.[45] First Isaiah seemed to lack reference to *berith*. Passages where it occurred were either not authentic (i.e., not from the prophet), or were non-religious in reference. However, First Isaiah speaks of Yahveh's determination to complete his purposes through his people, despite their stubbornness. This gives grounds for hope in the future.

Deuteronomy, where *berith* occurs frequently, moves the term in two directions: to refer to the Law, and to refer to the relationship between God and the people. Lohmeyer argues that Deuteronomy did not achieve what it aimed to do, and that it introduced a tendency for concentration upon the outer observance of the Law. The relationship of God to his people took on the nature of a treaty (*Vertrag*).

Jeremiah, for Lohmeyer, is a turning-point. Accepting the famous passage in Jeremiah 31.31-34 as coming from the prophet himself, Lohmeyer points to the mention in the passage of the forgiveness of sins (31.34). This can only be a one-sided act of graciousness, and takes the idea of *berith* into

---

[45] p.59, note 7

a new direction. In Second Isaiah *berith* occurs in parallelism with *hesed* (unfailing love), e.g., Isaiah 55.3, and the connection with *berith* as embodying the eternal purpose of God is strengthened:

> [Second Isaiah] speaks, as do also Jeremiah and Ezekiel, of the eternal *berith* of the future, and the realm of peace and grace.[46]

A universal widening of the notion of *berith* is found in the Psalms.

In the summary of the Old Testament material, Lohmeyer says that one can trace a process in which the profane uses of *berith* are replaced by the religious sense, and that the idea of *berith* as including mutual responsibility also fades into the background. This is the prelude to Chapter 3, which examines the use of *Diatheke* in the Septuagint.

Lohmeyer observes that when something is translated into another language, it is the shared assumptions in the target (i.e., the translator's) language that determine the meaning of a given word. Because there is no evidence in Greek that *Diatheke* could mean 'covenant' with its mutual obligations, it must mean in the Greek Old Testament something like *Verfügung* (power of disposition).[47] A difficulty for this argument arises from the fact that *Diatheke* is used to translate the Hebrew *berith* in passages where the *berith* refers to profane covenants with mutual obligations (an example would be I Samuel 18:3, the covenant between David and Jonathan). Lohmeyer brushed this difficulty aside. The instances were too few to be decisive.[48] A consideration of the

---

[46] [Second Isaiah] redet ebenso mit Jeremia und Ezechiel von der ewigen Berith der Zukunft, dem Reiche des Friedens und der Gnade. p.72.
[47] p.58
[48] p.93

fact that other Greek translations of the Greek Old Testament, particularly Aquila and Symmachus, who sometimes rendered *berith* as *Suntheke* (compact, treaty), brought the conclusion that this did not fundamentally alter the religious sense of *Diatheke* as' testament' or 'power of disposition'.[49]

Chapter 4 is devoted to 'Late Judaism' texts, such as the Apocrypha and Pseudepigrapha and Philo. It is in this chapter that Lohmeyer discusses the use of *berith* in the so-called 'Damascus Document' or 'Damascus Apocalypse', as he called it. Lohmeyer holds the view that the text was written in the Maccabean period in Damascus. He notes that the occurrence of *berith* some thirty-five times outstrips any book in the Old Testament. The fact that it has the phrase 'New Testament' (*berith hadashah*) makes it of special importance for the New Testament. *Berith* in the Damascus Apocalypse has nothing to do with mutual obligations. It refers to God's promises, the expression of God's will, and God's law.[50] Those who enter the 'New Testament' do so because of the future hopes in the coming of the Messiah, who is identical with 'the teacher of righteousness'. Lohmeyer concludes:

> that the longing expectation for the coming of the Messiah is identical to that of the Teacher of Righteous-ness, makes the pious [members of the fellowship] 'members of the new berith'. This is itself not yet historical reality, but a longed-for event of the future. [51]

Lohmeyer's treatment of the New Testament deals with Paul, Hebrews, Luke and the Last Supper Words of Institution. For

---

[49] p.107
[50] p.117
[51] 'Dass die Sehnsuchtige Erwartung auf das Kommen des Messias, mit dem der "Lehrer der Gerechtigkeit" identisch ist, die Frommen zu "Genossen der neuen Berith" macht, diese selbst also noch nicht geschichtliche Wirklichkeit, sondern ein ersehntes Ereignis der Zukunft ist', p.119

Paul, *diatheke* is concerned with the new order, instigated by the death of Jesus and characterised by the gift of the Spirit. It cannot be a covenant with mutual obligations. The same conclusion is reached via a different route from Hebrews. For the Last Supper, the crucial saying is the saying over the Cup (Mark 14:24) and the words, 'which is poured out for many'. Although Lohmeyer believed that the additional words in Matthew 26:28, 'for the forgiveness of sins', were an addition, he regarded them as adding the correct meaning.[52] The words of Jesus at the Last Supper came from the conviction of his Messiahship,[53] and made actual what for Jeremiah 31:31-34 could only have been a vision whose fulfilment was vague. The rendering 'testament' conveyed more adequately than 'covenant' the religious sense of *diatheke*. A Greek word that in its Hellenistic context was essentially a legal term having to do with the testamentary disposition of property, had become in the New Testament the heir to a prophetic religious sense, whose high point in Jeremiah 31:31-34, reinforced by the use of *berith* in the Damascus Apocalypse, described the new order instituted by God's grace in the death of Jesus.

It was said at the beginning of this chapter that *Diatheke* shows no trace of the influence of Hönigswald. There is one passage, however, that may indicate why Lohmeyer would find Hönigswald's *Denkpsychologie* method attractive. It reads as follows in a discussion of Paul:

> It agrees with the previous definition of the term completely, that its content, the centre of Christianity, the foundation of salvation, is given and is the basis of faith alone. What is new is that this *diatheke* should first become real in Abraham. Thus the opposition between 'new *diatheke*' and 'old *diatheke*' rests upon a terminological, not

---

[52] See p.160, note 2
[53] p.161, note 4

a temporal distinction, as the adjective 'old' might suggest.[54]

One notes here the words *Bestimmung* and *Begriff* and the suggestion that contained in the *Begriff* of the old covenant as established in Abraham (Genesis 15.6) was the importance of justifying faith in the promises of God; that the difference between the 'Old and the New Covenant' had less to do with time and more to do with *Begriff*. After Lohmeyer's contact with Hönigswald's philosophy, this type of argument and approach would become typical and unique for Lohmeyer.

---

[54] 'Es stimmt mit der bisherigen Bestimmung des Begriffes überein, dass als ihr Inhalt der Kern des Christentums, die Begründung des Heils allein auf den Glauben angegeben wird. Aber neu ist, dass diese *diatheke* schon in Abraham erstmal wirklich geworden sein soll. Dadurch wird der Gegensatz zwischen *kaine diatheke* ... und *palaia diatheke* auf einen rein begrifflichen, nicht auf zeitlichen, was in dem Attribute *palaia* zuliegen scheint, zurückgeführt', p.139.

CHAPTER FOUR

Soziale Fragen

Eight years separated the publication of *Diatheke* from the *Soziale Fragen im Urchristentum* (*Social Questions in Early Christianity*), which appeared in 1921.[55] During these eight years, Europe in general and Germany in particular had changed out of all recognition. The First World War had killed millions of young men, or had inserted into the post-war period men whose bodies and/or minds had been maimed by the war. Mothers, wives, fiancées and children had been left to grieve their menfolk. In Germany, the grandiose period following the establishment of the German Empire in 1870 and its industrial revolution had been replaced by a country marked by turmoil and upheaval, in which stability would only be re-established by the coming to power of the National Socialist party in 1933.

It is impossible for someone brought up in Britain to begin to understand what it meant for intellectual Germans such as Lohmeyer to come to terms with Germany's defeat in the war. Lohmeyer had served with distinction throughout the war and had apparently expected a German victory following its spring offensive in 1918.[56] He had also managed to continue his academic work to the point of completing a Habilitation thesis. Although it is said that his basic beliefs had not been

---

[55] E. Lohmeyer, *Soziale Fragen im Urchristentum*, Leipzig: Wissenschaft und Bildung 172, 1921. Reference is made here to the photographic reprint, Darmstadt: Wissenschaftliche Buchgesellschaft, 1973.
[56] Köhn, pp.9-10

altered by the war and the German defeat,[57] it is hard to imagine that Lohmeyer was in no way affected; and his later sympathy for Stefan George's vision of a New Germany, based upon poetic cultural values, may have owed something to the experience of the war and its aftermath.

Lohmeyer's *Soziale Fragen* is important for the present work in the following ways. First, it is a reminder of how far ahead of his New Testament colleagues he in fact was. The topic of the social background of Christianity became big business, especially in Anglo-American scholarship in the 1980s, helped by the work of the German scholar Gerd Theissen. Lohmeyer was 60 years ahead of this.

Secondly, it is clear from the introduction to *Soziale Fragen* that Lohmeyer was concerned for the post-war development of Germany. In 1929 he would contribute an essay to the volume edited by Paul Tillich and arising from the Kairos Group, with its commitment to social democracy. This suggests more than indifference to the outcome of the war.

Thirdly, *Soziale Fragen* is important for its treatment of Early Christianity, something that would become one of Lohmeyer's trademarks. A planned multi-volume approach to the subject was frustrated by the political situation and demands of the 1930s, the Second World War, and Lohmeyer's tragic death in 1946. Only the first volume was published (see below, p.123).

There have been many attempts to reconstruct the life of Jesus, some of them with the intention of trying to prove that the 'Jesus of history' was quite different from the 'Christ of faith' or that of the Early Church and subsequent Christian belief.

---

[57] Köhn p.10, and see note 38 for remarks of Tillich and Barth about how they felt.

What cannot be denied is that something that can be identified as 'Early Christianity' entered the stage of world history in the first century AD, something that left its mark in what is called the New Testament. To investigate this phenomenon, as opposed to trying to reconstruct the Jesus of history, seems to be methodologically unimpeachable, and it is a pity that more use has not been made of this kind of approach.

Soziale Fragen begins with the claim that there are similarities between the Roman-Hellenistic situation in which Early Christianity took its rise, and the post-war situation in which Lohmeyer is writing. Little is said about the latter, presumably because German readers in 1921 did not need to be reminded about their situation. By the parallel at the beginning of the first century AD, Lohmeyer seems to have had in mind the breakdown of the influence of the Greek city-states. An interesting observation is that 'history ... does not explain the life of the present, but the present indeed vivifies the understanding of history'.[58] Lohmeyer had not yet arrived at Hönigswald's view of the relation between past and present, but his observation is interesting for a biblical scholar.

Lohmeyer is at pains to distinguish and to distance himself from the view that it is material factors, especially the economy, which drive social development and produce new social movements. It is more complicated than that; and it is easy to see how Lohmeyer would find himself attracted to Hönigswald's refusal to explain things in mono-causal terms. The discussion of the mutual relationships between the state, the Church and the community, especially the family, stresses the importance of the community and its potential creativity, which in turn can have a reciprocal effect upon the state and

---

[58] *Soziale Fragen*, p.6, 'nicht ... deutet Geschichte das Leben der Gegenwart, wohl aber verlebendigt die Gegenwart die Erkenntnis der Geschichte'.

religion. It was this factor, embodied in the new dynamic of the Early Christian community, that Lohmeyer saw as the decisive social factor. Early Christianity, embedded in its world, was not simply a product of social and economic forces, but had its own creative part to play in perfecting the world in which it originated. In connection with Lohmeyer's later adoption of Hönigswald's ideas, it is noteworthy that Lohmeyer had sections devoted to discussion of the terms (*Begriffe*) *sozial* and *Gesellschaft* (community), without employing the logical rigour to their analysis that would become a feature of his work a little later.

Two sections were devoted, respectively, to the Hellenistic world and to the Roman world. The tendencies that followed the loss of Greek independence and the spread of Hellenistic culture had been reinforced by the rise of Roman rule. The landowners largely rented out their land to smallholders, and lived off the income. Here was a bureaucratic class at its most complete in Egypt. The real economic power lay with a minor bourgeoisie of manufacturers and traders, with sea-ports such as Corinth being especially important. Lohmeyer quoted Plato's complaint that the 'sea was the teacher of everything evil'.[59] The underclass consisted of slaves and day labourers who worked on estates. Slavery was a complex phenomenon, ranging from slaves who were integral parts of patrician families, to slaves who were employed in manufacturing trades and who were an economic threat to day labourers. Political power went hand in hand with property ownership and thus with alliances between petty monarchs and landowners. The other social classes were mostly apolitical. Among the land-owning groups the family as such was not a close-knit unit with mutual obligations, but a unit whose moral standards were, from a modern viewpoint, lax.

---

[59] *Soziale Fragen*, p.27, 'Die See ist Lehererin alles Bösen'.

The apolitical and somewhat philistine (Lohmeyer used the term, *Banause*) stance of the manufacturers and traders and lower classes led to a spiritual emptiness. This was not entirely satisfied by Stoic philosophy. Various eastern cults and mystery religions satisfied those who sought spiritual fulfilment. This was the world in which Early Christianity would develop and grow.

Lohmeyer frequently noted differences between the social and economic conditions of the Roman-Hellenistic world and those of his own situation, to some extent undermining his claim in the introduction that there were sufficient similarities to justify the treatment that he was undertaking. Judaism was thoroughly impregnated with Hellenistic ideas and culture, and Jews were scattered throughout what became the Roman Empire; yet they remained a distinctive group, bound together by their history and by their characteristic religious observances, including circumcision and Sabbath observance. In Palestine itself, the aristocratic and wealthy Sadducees exercised considerable power in alliance with petty monarchs and the later Roman rulers. Their wealth and power reinforced among the general population a theme found especially in the Psalms, that wealth and godlessness went together, as did poverty and the fear of God. The Pharisees were drawn from a lower class, including traders and craftsmen. They travelled widely in pursuit of their trading, but sought to be different from the rest of the population in their pursuit of applying Levitical standards of purity to their everyday lives. Jews who did not do this were regarded as ignorant lawbreakers of the divine law. The Essenes took Pharisaic ideals to the point where they avoided all contact with the world as much as possible, living in communities near the Dead Sea and possibly practising a community ownership of goods.

Palestine was a predominantly agricultural society, probably largely self-sufficient. Lohmeyer drew upon the parables of Jesus to point out the existence of slaves and day labourers in the society of his day, all of whom were dependent upon the generosity, or lack of it, of the employers and land-owners. However, there was no social unrest. Where there was resentment by the poor against the rich, this derived not from social but from religious causes:

> The burning social questions were drawn into the much deeper riddle of the unconditional divine affirmation of justice, and found an ultimate solution in trust based on knowledge of God and a longing for the divine presence.[60]

The chapter on the Hellenistic and Roman worlds was followed by a chapter entitled 'Early Christianity', whose first section dealt with Jesus. Up to now, Lohmeyer's style had been measured and scholarly. The section on Jesus is no less scholarly; but it is marked by a sense of excitement that makes it hard to avoid the feeling that Lohmeyer was being inspired by the kind of outlook found in Gundolf's interpretation of Stefan George. We find language similar to that of Gundolf when Lohmeyer describes the attitude of Jesus to the world, in which he sees himself as grounded in an unconditional 'Yes', implying a 'No' to the world.[61] That 'Yes' was alive in the heart of Jesus, who himself embodied it. He had come to light a fire on the earth, a fire kindled in heaven, a fire that aimed to transform human souls under the key words 'grace' and 'love', notions that would find expression in a new kind of community, the kingdom of God, which was a reality in the present as well as in the future. The forces shaping and

---

[60] *Soziale Fragen*, p.62, 'Die brennenden sozialen Fragen sind in dem weit tieferen Rätsel der unbedingt bejahten Gerechtigkeit Gottes aufgegangen und haben mit ihm in einem gottesgewissen Vertrauen und einer gottesnahen Sehnsucht ihre letzte Lösung gefunden'.
[61] *Soziale Fragen*, p.64

empowering this new community would shatter all the boundaries that determined normal human social life. It was not a matter of enhancing or fulfilling that normal social life. The message of Jesus had to do with salvation, something that breached the limitations of human restraint.

The fact that in the presence of Jesus a new, heavenly, reality had been manifested did not mean a denial of the world. Rather, the world was taken up in a new way into the new manifestation of the divine:

> In him the earth and the world are not denied but in the well-known double sense of the word taken up into something different, something divine, something other worldly.[62]

Corresponding to the 'inner' message of Jesus which was strange to the world (*erdfremd*) and above it (*überweltlich*) was his 'outer' life which eschewed, when his ministry began, any fixed place of abode and all embeddedness in any social class. He was unmarried, and freed himself from close family ties. While he had grown up among traders and craftsmen, his contacts were wide enough to reach on the one hand to the Pharisees, and on the other hand the despised 'people of the land' ('*amme ha`aretz*). While he had no doubt accepted the traditional equation of the rich with the godless, and the poor with the God-fearing, his message did not come from a proletarian hatred of other classes that sought the overthrow of the prevailing social and economic order. Lohmeyer noted the importance of the support Jesus received from women.[63]

---

[62] *Soziale Fragen*, p.66, 'In ihm wird Erde und Welt nicht verneint, aber in dem bekannten Doppelsinn des Wortes aufgehoben in einem Andern, Göttlichen, Überweltlichen'.
[63] *Soziale Fragen*, p.70

Jesus's message of the Kingdom of God demanded the existence of a new kind of life in community, one in which the ties of family were replaced by a sense of mutual belonging, based upon God's mercy. Such a way of life had no place for coercion or the enforcement of claims by law, no need for vows, no place for war. It was a love of the world as though it were not the world. It was an overcoming of the contra-dictions of life through the solution offered by God in the breaking-in of the last days into the present time.[64] Where love was supreme, there were no longer masters and servants. Action was not to be calculating in terms of means and ends, or profit and loss. Love brought with it a certain recklessness. The task left to the Early Church after the death of Jesus was to realise the vision and task that his own life had so clearly displayed.

The importance of this section on Jesus cannot be overestimated. It tells us how Lohmeyer, at the beginning of his work as a New Testament professor, understood Jesus; although, perhaps because of the audience Lohmeyer was addressing, it said nothing about Jesus as the Messiah or the eschatological Son of Man. It saw Jesus proclaiming and embodying in his ministry a new concept of the reality of God's kingdom breaking into the world. Jesus was fully conscious of his role as the way in which God's kingdom was being realised. He stood in the line of Old Testament prophets, but he was more than a prophet.

Lohmeyer was also clear that Jesus, before his death, had instituted a community meal that symbolised his flesh and blood, that is, the complete humanity of Jesus in which the fullness of God's grace was embodied.[65] This meal was to be

---

[64] *Soziale Fragen*, p.73
[65] *Soziale Fragen*, p.79

the central act, around which the building of the Christian community would take place, a new celebration of the community's unique life. It was this meal, together with the Early Christians' belief in the resurrection of Jesus, that prevented Christianity from becoming merely a backward-looking nostalgia to the time when Jesus had been alive, and impelled the first believers to realise, and to seek to communicate to others, their certainty that that future hope had become a present possibility.

Lohmeyer briefly sketched the development of the earliest Church from its first evangelistic, itinerant phase to its establishment in cities, the development of an apostolate, and the attempts described in Acts 4-5 to establish a community of goods based upon love. Although the Early Church was initially a sect within Judaism, it inevitably attracted the hostile attention of the Jewish authorities. Lohmeyer followed this brief section on the earliest community with a substantial section on Paul.

The latter section is important, because it makes it possible to compare Lohmeyer's views on Paul in 1921 with his views some years later. While it may again be necessary to make allowances for the readership Lohmeyer was addressing, at first sight this is a very different view of Paul compared with Lohmeyer's later thought. Lohmeyer argues that Paul rationalised the essential irrationality of the Gospel, as preached by Jesus, in three ways: by attempting a theodicy, by having an eschatological longing, and by having a mystical certainty of the possession of the Holy Spirit. By 'theodicy', Lohmeyer means that Paul attributed all suffering and injustice to the complete corruption of everything created.[66] Salvation was entirely dependent upon the predestinarian will

---

[66] *Soziale Fragen*, p.86, 'Die völlige Verderbtheit alles Kreatürlichen'.

of a hidden, transcendent God. Jesus had been transformed into the unreachable divinity of a heavenly lord, although he could also be a living and redeeming power in the heart of believers. The 'absence' of Jesus and his presence in the hearts of believers is spanned by the hope of the imminent return of Jesus. The Holy Spirit enables the power of Jesus, once manifested in history, to be present in the Early Christian community. As to Paul's social setting, his contacts were with the small traders and craftsmen and house slaves. There seemed to be no contact with educated members of the Hellenistic world. Educated people such as Apollos were Hellenistically sophisticated Jews.

An important difference between Jesus and Paul is that while Jesus saw everything from God's point of view, Paul saw everything from an earthly perspective. This resulted, among other things, in Paul being unable to implement that imperative of Jesus in which all differences between human beings were extinguished by the overwhelming grace of God. Further, an element of needing to achieve the divine fulfilment in the present world by human effort was introduced. Lohmeyer cited Philippians 3.12: 'Not that I have already obtained … but I press on', which opened Early Christianity to a new type of asceticism. However, and paradoxically, belief in the gift of the Holy Spirit enabled these tensions to be partly resolved. The Spirit enabled Christians to be 'in Christ', and for the community to be a temple of the Spirit.

Paul's attitude to social institutions was that of a traditional Hellenistic Jew of his day. The family was important, as was the state. Outwardly, the Christian congregations founded by Paul became organisations among other organisations. They were quite different from the communities implied in the teaching of Jesus, for all that they sought to honour Jesus as their heavenly Lord. Yet the irrational impulses of the Gospel proclaimed by Jesus were not entirely lost.

Lohmeyer's sketch of the period from Paul to the end of Early Christianity in the middle of the second century AD indicated how the impetus from Jesus had affected the development of the Christian communities. These communities had become situated in towns, they became increasingly ethnically diverse, and women played an important part in them. The underlying factor in this diversity was a sense that, like the people of God in the Old Testament, Christians were a chosen people. There was an adoption of the belief that the poor were closer to being godly than the rich, so that although work within the broad social class of small traders and craft workers was encouraged, the accumulation of wealth was discouraged. Simple lifestyles were the ideal, and surplus wealth was to be used to support the poor and unemployed members of the congregation.

Within congregations, a distinctive type of leadership, vested in the episcopal and diaconical offices, was meant to ensure that the congregation was a universal brotherhood embodying the Gospel of Jesus:

> It presents in time and space the wonder of the incarnation of the eternal Word, so that the burning longing for the end of time is transformed into the present apprehension of the life of God streaming into the community and its office.[67]

The irrational aspect of the teaching of Jesus was particularly apparent in the family. The Early Christians held to the Jewish

---

[67] *Soziale Fragen*, p.111, 'Es vergegenwärtigt in Zeit und Raum das Wunder der Menschwerdung des ewigen Logos, so dass die glühende Sehnsucht zum Ende der Zeit sich wandelt in das gegenwärtige Anschauen des in Gemeinde und Amt strömenden Leben Gottes'.

values of monogamy, faithfulness and marriage, as opposed to the more lax attitude of the Roman-Hellenistic world. Judaism was in theory, of course, polygamous, but in practice monogamous. But within the Christian family loyalty was the sense of the family connectedness of all Christian believers, and the belief that the family was not an end in itself but a means to serving God in the world. Thus, chastity and virginity became important means of using family ties to serve God's wider purposes.

Two writings, in their different ways, also expressed aspects of the message of Jesus. The Book of Revelation took up the 'enmity to the earth' aspect of the Gospel, uniting it with the eschatological hope of the return of the Lord. The 'earth' and its history were described in terms of a cosmic drama, whose 'end' lay in the fulfilment of God's purposes in Jesus. The Gospel of John, on the other hand, saw Jesus as the Word made flesh. His unique life was that of God and the bringer of salvation. In this way, the Early Christian movement turned, at the end of its course, back to its beginnings again.

Returning to social matters, Lohmeyer noted that the Christian communities remained rooted in the ambit of small traders and craft workers. There was no move to occupy public positions in government or administration, no move into academic or intellectual circles, and certainly no military involvement. The greater freedom created by the Roman Empire enabled the Christian communities to expand; but in one respect there was bound to be conflict. The Christian community could not accept the Emperor cult, the worship of the Emperor as divine. This brought Christians into conflict from time to time when public honouring of the Emperor was required. Christians could acknowledge only Jesus as the divine Lord.

In summing up, Lohmeyer returned to the unique and unrepeatable figure of Jesus as the basis for the social developments he had described. What was irrational in the message of Jesus had to be rationalised and socialised by the Early Church; but the paradox implied in this process had remained. Lohmeyer's *Soziale Fragen* is quite different from recent essays in this genre, especially those that have sought to portray Jesus as a kind social reformer and critic of his day.

CHAPTER FIVE

Vom Begriff der religiösen Gemeinschaft

Only four years separated Lohmeyer's *Soziale Fragen* (1921) from his *Vom Begriff der religiösen Gemeinschaft* (*On the Notion of a Religious Community*) (1925), but in that time he had mastered Hönigswald's philosophy and had learned to use it to express his unique understanding of the New Testament and the Early Christianity to which it bore witness. This is evident in several ways.

First, *Vom Begriff der religiösen Gemeinschaft* was published in a series edited by Hönigswald and entitled *Wissenschaftliche Grundfragen (Basic Scientific Questions)*.[68] Those associated with the series included the philosophers Bruno Bauch and Ernst Cassirer, the anatomist Ernst Kallius, the mathematician Adolf Kneser and the psychiatrist Oswald Bunker. The aim of the series was to explore philosophically the fundamental questions that individual disciplines had to address in order to be scientific (*wissenschaftlich*).[69]

Secondly, there were, among the footnotes, references to Hönigswald's *Philosophie des Altertums* (2nd ed., 1920, see Lohmeyer, p.1) and *Grundlagen der Denkpsychologie* (2nd ed.,

---

[68] E. Lohmeyer, *Vom Begriff der religiösen Gemeinschaft*, in R. Hönigswald (ed.), *Wissenschaftliche Grundfragen. Philosophische Abhandlungen* III, Leipzig: Verlag B. G. Teubner, 1925.

[69] See the note by Hönigswald setting out the aims of the series in the inside cover of the Lohmeyer volume.

1925, see Lohmeyer, p.41). The technical term 'monad', so important for Hönigswald's system, was used on page 38. Thirdly, the declared aim of his work, as adumbrated in the introduction, was to investigate those philosophical questions that were fundamental and common to all scientific disciplines. In the case of the religious matters discussed in Lohmeyer's monograph, the task was not so much to try to reconstruct past history as to discover

> [i]n the flux of the historical appearances the permanence of the factual content; in the passing phases of the historical forms, the abiding features of all religious problems.[70]

This would mean that the book was critical-historical, not historical-critical, in the sense that an historical investigation was subjected to philosophical critical scrutiny. Lohmeyer quoted a well-known phrase of Goethe about discovering the general in the particular case, or seeing in the particular case an instance of what was general.

The fact that general principles underlying all scientific investigations were being explored in the series did not mean that all scientific disciplines were being reduced to one, as in the Neo-Kantian attempt to reduce all disciplines to mathematics. Fundamental to Hönigswald's thought, as was argued in chapter one, was the uniqueness of each discipline, even if their basic philosophical problems were similar. In Lohmeyer's contribution to the series, the religious community that was investigated was exemplified in the Early Christian community, for whom the figure of Jesus was crucial and central. As in *Soziale Fragen*, it was assumed that the figure of Jesus as witnessed to in the Gospels was sufficiently clear to

---

[70] *Vom Begriff*, p.2: 'In dem Wandel der historischen Erscheinungen die Unwandelbarkeit des sachlichen Gehaltes, in der Vergänglichkeit der geschichtlichen Formen die Unvergänglichkeit der religiösen Probleme'.

enable a whole philosophical structure to be built on his uniqueness.

The book begins with a discussion of the terms found in the New Testament by which the Christian community is described, or describes itself, beginning with the terms 'disciple', and 'teacher'. In the Early Christian community these terms had a special meaning, because the relationship between Jesus and his followers was not that of the usual teacher and his students. Jesus did not *teach* the truth; he *was* the truth so that those who became his disciples were invited not to *learn* from him but to *follow* him. This fact profoundly affected the nature of the Early Christian community. Its members were bound together by being not in a dialogic relationship with their master, that is, a relationship of exploration of knowledge by questions and answers, but by being in a monologic relationship, that is, one in which Jesus was accepted in faith as being himself the truth.

After the death of Jesus, the Christian community was often referred to as 'saints' (Greek *hagioi*).[71] Lohmeyer emphasised that 'holiness' in this context was not an ethical aspiration towards which believers must strive, but something given. It was a being taken from the sphere of 'sin' into an 'inviolable actuality',[72] which was contained in the notion of faith. For the moment, no attempt will be made to spell out this last point further. There is much about the nature and function of faith later in the work.

Holiness also implies a sense of fulfilment that gathers up the chaotic and fragmented pieces of history into a meaningful whole, because history is seen from God's point of view. To

---

[71] Lohmeyer gives ten references from Acts, Romans and I Corinthians, concluding with 'and often'. *Vom Begriff*, p.12, note 25.

[72] *Vom Begriff*, p.12, 'eine unerschütterliche Tatsächlichkeit'.

the extent that Early Christian believers are 'saints', they are also gathered up into this totality. This is one of the distinctive features of the religious community that Lohmeyer is analysing. In its existence in space and time, that community of 'saints' manifests and puts into action the eternal truths which give rise to its existence. Further, because it is constituted by God's action, its members do not depend upon human ideas of belonging or hierarchy. Lohmeyer refers to Colossians 3.11: 'There is neither Greek nor Jew, circumcised, nor uncircumcised, barbarian, Scythian, slave or free, but Christ is all and in all'.

A new section entitled *Die Norm der Gesellschaft* (*The Norm of the Community*) (pp.22-35) deals especially with faith. It starts from Jesus's command that people should repent and believe. Belief is connected to proclamation. The proclamation is believed, that is, it is experienced (*erlebt*), and experiencing means that reality is seen in the light of the Kingdom of God. This means that although the act of believing is essentially an individual thing (Lohmeyer speaks of the monadic structure of believing), it can only be realised in the corporate dimension of the Kingdom of God. Belief is not transferable from one person to another; but it is the existence of the Kingdom of God that enables people to come to faith.

A complicated discussion explores the difference between faith and knowledge. Knowledge presupposes an exploration of the conditions (*Bedingungen*) that make possible the existence and apprehension of objects (*Gegenstände*). Faith is an apprehension of what is unconditioned (*das Unbedingte*) that lifts the individual to a unique experience of religious reality. It is an apprehension of God in a complete unconnectedness from the world, which at the same time imparts a unity to all that exists. Lohmeyer sums this up as follows:

> Here…an Unconditioned is the final 'ground' of all preaching that is experienced, indeed, in what is conditional, but is not graspable in what is conditional or explicable through what is conditional.[73]

The question of Jesus, 'Do you believe?' implies that faith is present and active in the unity of the message and the proclamation.

This discussion is followed by a consideration of the notion, important for Lohmeyer's work, of eschatological determination, that is, the definition of the nature of things in relation to the last days or end of time that will discern the true meaning of all things. The Kingdom of God which Jesus proclaimed is always present and always immanent. There is a nice pun in the German on *da* (there) and *nah* (near). It binds together the present, past and future so that to believe in the proclamation of Jesus is to see things now in their completedness from the perspective of their eventual fulfilment.

The next section, 'The I and the community' (*Das Ich und die Gemeinschaft*), brings us closest to Lohmeyer's appropriation of Hönigswald's thought, and also helps us to see what it was about Lohmeyer's work that most puzzled and alienated his New Testament colleagues. It was pointed out in chapter one (p.22) how important the I-relationship (*Ich-Bezug*) was in Hönigswald's thought. In this section, Lohmeyer discusses the I-relationship in the light of the concept of faith. Two allusions to biblical passages show how far Lohmeyer was from

---

[73] *Vom Begriff*, p.24 'Hier … ist der letzte "Grund" aller Verkündigung ein Unbedingtes, das wohl am Bedingtheiten erlebbar, nicht aber in Bedingtheiten erfaßbar oder durch Bedingtheiten erklärbar ist'.

traditional New Testament exegesis. The first was an allusion to Romans 7, where Paul speaks of the internal conflict that he is experiencing or, according to another interpretation, had experienced, as he wrestled with the power of law-induced sin in his life. 'The good that I would I do not; the evil that I would not that I do' (Romans 7.15) is his classic statement of the dilemma and much ink has been spilled in discussion of it.

For Lohmeyer it is a manifestations of *Zweiseelenhaftigkeit*, his translation of the Greek word *dipsuxos* found in James 1.8 and rendered, for example, by the New English Bible as 'double-minded' and the Lutheran Bible as *unbeständig*.[74] In its context in James it seems to refer to a defect in a person's character – an unwillingness or inability to serve God with one's whole heart, mind and strength. Lohmeyer seems to understand it as arising from the tension that comes when the I-relationship of faith has to be held together with the I-relationship of normal experience, a factor that is discussed later in connection with the notion of the soul. He cites the experience of Augustine and Luther as well as that of Paul, but in those three cases the problem faced by the individuals concerned is surely not that of being reluctant to serve God, but the opposite: of wanting desperately to find a way to God. Neither can their experience be adequately understood in Lohmeyer's terms. As I see it, the certainty that the experience of faith brings in Lohmeyer's account ought not to lead to the desperate longings for faith exemplified in Augustine and Luther.

In discussing the soul, Lohmeyer seems to see it not in individual terms ('the notion is not so much ... to be seen as equivalent to individuality'),[75] but as referring to an inter-subjective factor bringing together those who have

---

[74] Lohmeyer's word means something like 'bound to two souls'.
[75] *Vom Begriff*, p.3, 'Der Begriff ist ebensowenig...mit dem der Individualität gleichzusetzen'.

experienced faith: 'It is the legitimacy of this experience itself'.[76] Indeed, Lohmeyer compares the soul with the monad which, in its uniqueness, is at the same time bound to an infinite number of other monads. There follows, in this connection, another important discussion of knowledge and faith in Hönigswaldian terms. All experience consists of a process of the I grasping and being grasped by an object that is thought. In the case of faith, the 'I' is grasped by and grasps that which is Unconditioned. This experience of God involves being grasped by God and being given meaning by God, and the notion of the soul is a description of that fact, realised in the individual, but linked to infinite numbers of others who have also been grasped by God.

Earlier, Lohmeyer had quoted, as exemplifying the notion of soul, the saying of Jesus, 'What shall it profit man if he gain the whole world and lose his soul?' (Mark 8.36), but this is hardly satisfactory. Lohmeyer's understanding of faith, based upon Hönigswald's theory of cognition, is striking and indeed persuasive, but that it bears any relation to the saying of Jesus in Mark 8.36 is most unlikely. The meaning of 'soul' in that saying has to be sought in Jewish and Greek technical vocabularies of the time of Jesus, and not on the basis of a vigorous philosophical investigation of the notion of faith, however illuminating that may be in itself.

The soul, according to Lohmeyer, is a representative of the religious community; but how does this square with instances of the isolation of the soul in the experience of believers and, in the case of Jesus, his aloneness in the Garden of Gethsemane and on the Cross? The problem is overcome as follows. To be in the relationship of faith with God means to be bound, in God, with other souls that are related to him.

---

[76] *Vom Begriff*, p.38, 'Sie ist die Gesetzlichkeit dieses Erlebens selbst'.

Aloneness does not necessarily contradict community, but rather confirms the force of the religious community, in that the soul needs the community in order to be meaningful in a religious sense.

The next main section, entitled 'Action in the Community' (pp.49-66), deals with love, which is the practical expression of belief. Belief brings with it not only a religious perspective, but also an ethical empowering. To believe means to act in a believing, that is, ethical, way. But the notion of love also entails further thinking about the concept of sin and holiness. 'Sin' becomes a way of describing the world and its standards, while holiness is what is given by God in the act of believing. Holiness is a religiously-implanted sense of obligation. This also impinges upon the world of nature which, according to Paul's insight in Romans 8.21, is in bondage to sin and awaits its exaltation to holiness, that is, its new creation. Yet nature can be seen by faith from the standpoint of holiness, and can thus impart experiences of deep religious significance.

Lohmeyer next deals with the problem that the forgiveness of sins, which in one sense happens only once, when the gift of faith lifts a person from sin to holiness, is also something that recurs in religious practice. This is because the believer has to exist, and can only exist, in the continuum of time, and is thus both holy and on the path to holiness. Lohmeyer warns against detaching the notion of holiness from its interlocking relationship with faith and its embeddedness in the community implied by faith, so that it becomes a 'reified substantiality'.[77]

Coming on to love, Lohmeyer emphasises that, like holiness, it is to be understood only within the structure of faith in the

---

[77] *Vom Begriff*, p.57, 'Eine verdingliche Substantialität'.

Unconditioned and the community which this entails. This is why, he argues, the New Testament uses the unusual Greek word *agape* and why, in the New Testament, it is described as something that knows no boundaries. Thus, one's neighbour is anyone in need, and the acts of love must involve doing such irrational things as loving one's enemies! Love, in the Early Christian understanding does not create a community; it represents a community that has been created by God. It became necessary, after the death of Jesus, for the Christian community to create boundaries in order to define itself and to distinguish between believers and non-believers; but this does not obscure the essential connection in Early Christianity between faith in the Unconditioned, and the unlimited demand of love that is the practical side of faith.

The final main section is entitled 'History and Community' (pp.66-86) and it is important because it is essential for understanding Lohmeyer's concept of history and eschatology. In language reminiscent of Hönigswald's observation on Genesis chapter 1, Lohmeyer points out the illogicality of speaking about the beginning and end of history, if history is thought of as measurable time. Something must strictly have come before it began, as something else must be there after it has ended. But from the standpoint of faith, beginning and end have meaning in that they indicate a divine perspective. Lohmeyer describes time and history as 'the buzzing loom on which the living garment of divinity is woven'.[78] Events of history are mere fragments, behind which a whole purpose can sometimes be glimpsed.

Lohmeyer emphasises that history must be seen not in the context of human understanding, but from the perspective of

---

[78] *Vom Begriff*, p.69, 'Der sausende Webstuhl, an dem der Gottheit lebendiges Kleid gewirkt wird'.

faith. The word 'now' must lie outside the dimension of measurable time. 'Just as in faith the 'I' is experienced as an expression of divinely composed and determined being, so also the 'now' of faith is experienced as an expression of the divine timelessness, in which the present is always at hand'.[79] It is essential to realise that when Lohmeyer uses the terms 'eschatology' and 'eschatological' as he does this in later works, he is not talking about measurable time and something that stands at the end of it. He is speaking about time seen from the perspective of faith, where what is 'last' is necessarily always present.

In the course of the development of Christianity the necessity to see time from the perspective of faith was lost. It was seen only from a knowledge point of view, and this led to the development of the Christian Church as a community within measurable time and its beginnings as an incident within measurable time. This idea led to the early Catholic development of a hierarchy in the Church, and to the idea that it represented in measurable time the Kingdom of God on earth. It was the appearance in the history of the Church of figures such Augustine and Luther that enabled the nature of faith not to be completely forgotten. What is unended in history is complete in God, and the individual 'I', anchored in history, attains after death the completeness that faith imparted and towards which the 'I' has been travelling.

Vom Begriff der religiösen Gemeinschaft is an impressive work, full of insight and inspiring thoughts. It is perhaps the clearest statement of Lohmeyer's own faith and experience of being grasped by the Unconditioned in an encounter as real as the

---

[79] *Vom Begriff*, p.71, 'Wie im Glauben das Ich als Ausdruck eines göttlichen Gesetzt- und Bestimmtseins erlebt wird, so wird auch der Jetzt des Glaubens als ein Ausdruck der göttlichen Zeitlosigkeit erlebt, in der "Gegenwärtigkeit" immer vorhanden ist'.

normal fact of empirical consciousness in which the 'I' grasps and is grasped by an object. Interestingly, Lohmeyer does not go on to posit metaphysical essences on the basis of faith. This would imply that faith was a kind of superior knowledge, whereas, as Lohmeyer made clear, the logical implications of faith and knowledge are quite different. His position is grounded, rather, in a kind of broad Neo-Kantianism as represented by Hönigswald. It is a kind of 'religionless Christianity' whose faith is positive and grounded in the uniqueness of the figure of Jesus, who is the truth and is more than a prophet. It is a tragedy that so many of his contemporaries found it hard, or even impossible, to understand what he was saying.

CHAPTER SIX

The Commentary on the Book
of Revelation

Hard on the heels of *Vom Begriff der religiösen Gemeinschaft* appeared Lohmeyer's commentary on the Book of Revelation, which he must have been working on at the same time that he was writing *Vom Begriff*.[80] There is one reference in the commentary to *Vom Begriff* (p.18), where Lohmeyer explains the term *ekklesia* as having a double sense: for the community of the saints (*Heilige*) and fulfilled (*Vollendete*), and the incomplete (*unvollkommen*) historical organised Church. It is significant that the commentary and *Vom Begriff* were running in parallel, because while the influence of Stefan George on the commentary is apparent, the influence of Hönigswald is equally important.

As was noted earlier, Lohmeyer did not impose the number seven on the Book of Revelation; it abounds in sevens. There are seven churches, and the one like the Son of Man appears in the midst of seven golden lampstands (1.12). A scroll has seven seals (5.1), there are seven angels with seven trumpets (8.6) and seven angels with seven plagues (15.1). An angel has seven bowls (17.1), and there is a scarlet beast with seven heads (17.3). But if the sevens were already there, Lohmeyer went further and imposed sevenfold patterns on the book,

---

[80] E. Lohmeyer, *Die Offenbarung des Johannes* (Handbuch zum Neuen Testament 16), Tübingen: J.J.C.B. Mohr, 1926. The preface is dated Christmas 1925.

dividing what he called the 'apocalyptic part' into seven main sections:

I   Seven seal visions (6.1 to 8.1)
II   Seven trumpet visions (8.2 to 11.15)
III Seven visions of the kingdom of the dragon
      (11.15 to 13.18)
IV Seven visions of the coming of the Son of
      Man (14.1-24)
V   Seven bowl visions (15.1 to 16.21)
VI Seven visions of the fall of Babylon
      (17.1 to 19.10)
VII Seven visions of the End (19.11 to 21.4)

The 'apocalyptic part', labelled D, is preceded by three parts: A proemium (1.1-2), B prologue (1.4-8), C the exhortatory part; and followed by three parts, E the promissory part (21.5 to 22.7), F the epilogue (22.8-19), and G the End (22.20-21). According to this scheme there are seven parts of which the fourth, D, is central, which is itself divided into seven sections, of which the fourth is central, dealing with the coming of the Son of Man.

As noted earlier, Stefan George's *The Seventh Ring* had been published in 1907 with the fourth part, that concerning Maximin being central. The idea of the ring, apparently, had to do with the ring in the trunks of trees by which their age could be told.[81] There can be little doubt that Lohmeyer's division of Revelation into its seven sections, with the fourth part being central, owed much to *The Seventh Ring*. However, Lohmeyer did not stop there. He divided the passage into strophes and poetic lines on the basis mostly of formal criteria. For example, the inaugural vision of chapter 4 is divided into seven strophes, each with seven lines (p.41) and the thrice-holy

---

[81] See E. Morwitz, *Kommentar zu dem Werk Stefan Georges*, Munich: Helmut Küpper, 1960, p.215.

acclamation of God is seen as sevenfold: holy, holy, holy, almighty, who was, who is, who is to come.

Lohmeyer's conviction of the importance of the number seven in Revelation led him to argue that it was a unified composition by a single author whose irregular Greek was partly that of a Semitic speaker, but also a special language necessary to convey the ideas contained in the book. Where other scholars had argued from inconsistencies and apparent contradictions for multiple sources or authors, Lohmeyer resolutely found ways of defending the unity of the book. An example is the problem of 21.5-8, where those who conquer are promised divine adoption, while the cowardly, faithless and other offenders will be cast into the lake of fire and sulphur. This seems to duplicate 19.17-21, where various classes of the ungodly are cast into the fiery lake, and to contradict 21.1-4, where the old has passed away and all things are become new. The apparent duplication and contradiction had prompted R.H. Charles, whose commentary was much used by Lohmeyer, to suggest that the original writer of the book had died and another author had written 21.5 to 22.7.[82] Lohmeyer argued that the difficulties disappear if it is assumed that 21.5 to 22.7 did not occur at the end of time, but were instruction, comfort and promise in and for the time of the seer.

One can be forgiven for seeing in Lohmeyer's argumentation a tendency to make the facts fit the theory. On the other hand, and in Lohmeyer's favour, is the fact that scholars who assumed that there were multiple sources and authors were likewise imposing upon the text an overall view of its origins

---

[82] Lohmeyer, *Offenbarung*, p.164, citing R. H. Charles, *A Critical and Exegetical Commentary on the Revelation of St John* (International Critical Commentary), Edinburgh: T. & T. Clark, 1920, vol. 2, pp.144ff.

and compilation. Lohmeyer may or may not have gone too far in treating Revelation as a unified poetic composition by an inspired prophet, but many of the features that he pointed out were arguably there in the text, and needing explanation.

Lohmeyer's view of Revelation as visionary poetry made him unsympathetic to attempts to find historical allusions in the book. A long excursus on chapter 17 argued against seeing in the chapter an allusion to Rome and to an Emperor Nero *redivivus*. It was not clear that the seven heads of the beast were seven Roman emperors and that the ten horns were ten satraps. The description of the king 'who was, and is not and will again be' (verse 10) was a demonic imitation of the divine title of the 'one who was, and is and is to come'. The more likely source for the vision was Daniel 7, with the beast of four heads and 10 horns (Daniel 7.5-7). Lohmeyer was also reluctant to identify the passage with the actual persecution of the Early Church. For example, in discussing Revelation 6.8, Lohmeyer argued that the seer was living between the memory of earlier persecutions and the prospect of future ones, but did not refer specifically to an actual persecution.

Lohmeyer was interested by the fact that only seven churches are addressed in the opening chapters, and that the Ephesian Church is mentioned first. He suggested that the seven churches represented the whole number of the congregations and that Ephesus came first, because it had assumed leadership among the congregations following the destruction of Jerusalem in AD 70.

The concluding pages of the book (pp.181-199) which are, in a sense, the introduction, make it clear why Lohmeyer was so unsympathetic to the usual scholarly attempts to find in Revelation allusions to recent persecutions of Christians, veiled references to historical persons such as Nero, and a view of the book as encouragement to a beleaguered and persecuted Church. To take this view was to place the book in the sphere of 'knowledge', with the apocalyptic images being a kind of superior metaphysical knowledge. In fact, Lohmeyer's understanding of the book is wholly determined by the position worked out in the previous book, *Vom Begriff der religiösen Gemeinschaft*. Faith *(Glaube)* is qualitatively different from knowledge. It is something experienced *(erlebt)*, which brings with it certainties which nonetheless have to be situated and lived within the dimensions of time and 'the world'. The 'eschatological drama' is in no way determined by historical events, but by the inner logic of the sinfulness of the world that is manifested as believers are made holy through the experience of faith. The manifestations of God and Christ are experienced through grace, and this faith experience gives new meaning to the ideas of time and eschatology. Lohmeyer writes of 'a faith-fulfilled present' *(eine glaubenserfüllte Gegenwart*, p.196) and defines eschatology as a 'symbolic putting into the end of the timeless meaning of belief' *(eine bildhafte "Verendzeitlichung" zeitlosen Glaubenssinnes*, p.196). The 'revelations' do not unveil or disclose anything that is not in principle already known, but testify to what is promised, what is 'known' through faith.

What, then, is the origin of the Book of Revelation? It is the work of someone with a priestly and literary background, possibly that of John the Presbyter mentioned by Papias. The material is traditional, drawn from the Old Testament and the wider piety of the Oriental world, for all that Lohmeyer sees it rooted in a kind of Jewish 'gnosis', rather than a Hellenistic milieu. Here it must be observed that in the main body of the commentary, the text of Revelation is richly illustrated by references to the Old Testament, its apocrypha and pseudepigrapha, and Rabbinic sources as well as the work of scholars such as Rudolf Bultmann on Mandaic literature, and Richard Reitzenstein on Greek aspects of Gnosticism and mystery religions. Yet, typically, and reminiscent of Hönigswald, Lohmeyer insists on the uniqueness of the compilation. Although he does not use the actual term 'monad', Lohmeyer expresses the idea in other language, for example, as he writes,

> So a new unity is created and formed in the figure of the seer. It is a unity, in which the 'outside' of the eschatology resembles the inside of faith; and it is a figure [of the seer] which, as the preacher of faith's present and future, is an eternal divine word.[83]

It was pointed out at the beginning of the chapter that Lohmeyer must at some stage have been working simultaneously on the commentary and on *Vom Begriff der religiösen Gemeinschaft*. It seems clear that the two works should be seen as complementary, the one providing the intellectual basis, the other (Revelation) spelling out in practice what faith meant in one example of the literature of the Early Church. With these two books Lohmeyer had reached the intellectual position that would underlie and shape his subsequent scholarly work.

---

[83] *Offenbarung*, p.198, 'So ist eine neue Einheit geschaffen und in dem Seher Gestalt geworden. Es ist eine Einheit, in der das "Draußen" der Eschatologie gleich dem Drinnen des Glaubens ist; und es ist eine Gestalt, die als Verkünder des Glaubens Gegenwart und Zukunft Prophet eines ewigen Gotteswortes ist'.

CHAPTER SEVEN

Kyrios Jesus

Kyrios Jesus, a detailed examination of Philippians 2.5-11, appeared in 1928.[84] It is one of the works of Lohmeyer to which frequent reference is still made, because Lohmeyer was the first scholar to suggest that the passage was a Christian psalm, which was quoted, but not composed, by Paul. It is a very complex piece of writing, full in its earlier pages of the dense reasoning that Lohmeyer had developed from his study of Hönigswald. It also displayed Lohmeyer's interest in poetic forms and structures.

The psalm, as Lohmeyer constantly called it, was divided by him poetically as follows (in my translation; Lohmeyer gave it in the Greek):

1. being in the form of God
he considered it not a prize
to be equal with God

2. but emptied himself
taking the form of a servant
becoming in the likeness of men

3. and being found in form like a man
he humbled himself
becoming obedient even to death [death of the cross]

---

[84] E. Lohmeyer, *Kyrios Jesus. Eine Untersuchung zu Phil. 2, 5-11.* Sitzungsberichte der Heidelberger Akademie der Wissenschaften, Philosophisch-historische Klasse, Jhrg. 1927/28, 4. Abhandlung. Reference is made here to the 2nd edition, Heidelberg: Carl Winter, 1961.

4. wherefore God highly exalted him
and conferred on him
the name above all names

5. so that at the name Jesus
every knee should bow
in heaven, and on earth, and below earth

6. and every tongue confess
that Jesus Christ is Lord
to the glory of God the Father

It will be noted that Lohmeyer bracketed the words 'death of the cross', because he held that they had been added to the poem by Paul in order to express Paul's especial concern for the Cross as the centre of his preaching (cf. I Corinthians 1.18). What made the passage so important was its lack of specific reference to the Cross, even though it was implied in the notion of obedience even to death.

In what can be defined as a sketch of the circumstances in which the poem originated in Early Christianity (pp.85-89), Lohmeyer described the situation in Judaism, represented by apocalyptic, in which the evil of the world had become increasingly apparent. God himself had been felt to be more remote, and apocalyptic hopes of a divine intervention in the form of a Son of Man and the coming of the end of time had gained strength. The Early Church had come to believe that, in Jesus, the Son of Man had indeed come, bringing the end of time, but not in the way they expected. There were several attempts to account for what had occurred in the Jesus event, accounts which drew upon parts of the Old Testament and salvation beliefs of the time, so as to find adequate language to describe the unique experience of the Early Church.

Lohmeyer saw in the Letter to the Hebrews one such attempt (pp.77-83), and other attempts in the Book of Revelation and

John's Gospel. The poem in Philippians 2.5-11, perhaps originating in Antioch, was the earliest such attempt, and was closer to Johannine thought than Pauline thought, albeit quoted by Paul.

The three stanzas could be seen as thesis, antithesis and synthesis (p .30). The first was situated in the heavenly realm, the second in the earthly, the third in the exaltation from the earthly to the heavenly. The poem was initially the result of theological *thinking* (p.14), and to this extent could be subjected to philosophical analysis before the effects of believing (*Glauben*) were examined. As a general observation, the poem dealt with the difference between divinity and humanity, not in the sense of sinfulness versus holiness, transience versus permanence, or weakness versus strength, but in terms of the form (*Gestalt*) which divinity and humanity respectively took (p.14). Divine form belonged to the sphere of being, whereas the form of humanity belonged to the sphere of becoming and dying. In turn, the form (*Gestalt*) was defined and determined by action (*die Tat*). A form was what it did.

This brings Lohmeyer to allude to biology and the relationship between existence (*Bestand*) and achievement (*Leistung*), and it is difficult here not to recall that Hönigswald had been impressed by the vitalism theory of Hans Driesch (see above p.20). However, Lohmeyer makes the allusion in order to emphasise that in the idea of the form (*Gestalt*), as he understands it, he is not thinking of a development natural to an organism, but of a religious-ethical factor which is a fundamental property of form and not separable from it. This enables Lohmeyer to posit a divine existence that is purely religious-ethical action (*Tat*). The opposite of this is human existence which is defined not by action (*Tat*), but by endeavour (*Tun*) which belongs to the sphere of becoming and dying. Thus Lohmeyer believes that the antithesis between God and humanity and heaven and earth are implicit in the notion of form (*Gestalt*) as applied to the divine and the human, and that this theoretical assumption is the necessary background for interpreting the poem. This affects the way in which the words about being 'equal with God' are to be understood. They belong to the sphere of ethical decision-making if the 'form' of God is understood in ethical-religious terms.

In the first stanza the words, 'being in the form of God', are remarkable because they do not occur in the Old Testament. God's revelations there and those of his angels do not take any concrete form but are formless in wind, cloud, smoke, fire and so on. However, the words 'in the form of God' must be understood of the person so described as meaning that his being is inseparable from his religious-ethical nature. In this sense he is both 'equal with God' and yet separate from him (p.20).

The words about equality with God as 'not a prize to be grasped' raise logical questions. They imply a logical possibility that is expressed in later Jewish and Christian speculation about the devil as a fallen angel, who was cast out because he wished to be equal to God. On the other hand, not wanting to be equal with God can be seen as that ethical quality that is essential to divinity. Lohmeyer believes that these phrases and their contradictions reflect the logical implication of the fact that the notion of good is meaningless without the concept of evil, and that obedience is meaningless without the notion of temptation and wrongdoing. In other words, reality as understood from a human standpoint is dialectical in terms of good and evil and similar moral binary oppositions (pp.24-25). This necessary dialectical contradiction is overcome in faith. The experience of being grasped by the Unconditioned gives birth to the 'I' in a new way, and in the process the 'I' realises both that it is a new 'I' and also that the world is God's creation.[85] But, because faith overcomes the contradiction between good and evil, and implies the fact of temptation, it becomes bound up with the notion of faith.

There follows at this point in Lohmeyer's discussion an important comment on myth, whose nature is seen to be a description of fundamental truths in narratives set in primal time. One is reminded here of Lessing's observation in the *Education of the Human Race,* paragraph 48, when he speaks of 'the clothing of abstract truths ... in allegories and instructive circumstances, which were narrated in actual circumstances'.[86] Lohmeyer concludes that behind the phrase, 'did not consider it a prize to be grasped', is a cosmological myth about creation and temptation. What was the nature of the thing to be grasped? The phrase 'to be equal with God' cannot be speaking of *substance* but of function or power, as indicated in Genesis 3.5: 'You shall be like God, knowing good and evil' and the Temptations of Jesus (Matthew 4.1-11), where what is offered and sought is a share of God's ruling power (p.28). The New Testament implies that Satan has somehow come into possession of the power in the world, which God will bring to an end at the end of time.

This leads to the second stanza, which describes the entry of the One in divine form into the world of human existence. The much-discussed term 'emptied himself' cannot refer to his substance; nor is the form of the Emptied One an outer husk

---

[85] *Kyrios Jesus,* p.25, 'Weil er weiß, daß er eine neue Schöpfung ist, weiß er auch von der Schöpfung durch Gott'.

[86] G. E. Lessing, *Die Erziehung des Menschengeschlechts* in *Gotthold Ephraim Lessing Werke,* Darmstadt: Wissenschaftliche Buchgesellschaft, 1996, vol. 8, p.500; ET by F. W. Robertson, London: Anthroposophical Publishing Co., 1927, p.14

subject to change, housing an unchangeable 'inner'. 'In him, what is interior is also exterior and what is exterior is also interior'.[87] The emptying is a purely ethical act (*Tat*), but given that form (*Gestalt*) is inseparable from act (*Tat*), the act of complete renunciation of god-like power becomes or is itself, a form of divinity. Here the term 'servant', which Jesus becomes, takes on the double meaning of human humility and divine exaltation. Lohmeyer sees a connection with the Servant of God in Isaiah 53.

The third stanza carries the account of the earthly existence of the Emptied One to the point of his obedience unto death; and here Lohmeyer makes an observation that has been much commented on by later interpreters. He observes that the death of the servant is not the end of a life in the normal human sense. It is an ethical act, meant as the completion of the process of emptying. Such a decision for death can only be made by one 'in the form of God'.[88]

In this stanza the words 'like a man' also occur. Lohmeyer perceives behind the Greek the Aramaic *k^{e}bar-nash*, 'like a son of man', and a reference to the Son of Man known from Daniel 7.13 and I Enoch 46.5, 48.2. The words 'becoming obedient' imply a divine law, because obeying has to do with obeying the law. In this case, there is implied a divine law (*Gesetz Gottes*) that the path to the highest position of lordship is that of obedience unto death. Returning to the unnatural nature of the servant's death, Lohmeyer sees in it a descent to the world of the dead, indicated by his exalted lordship 'beneath the earth', as well as on earth and in heaven.

---

[87] *Kyrios Jesus*, p.34, 'In ihm, was innen ist, auch außen und, was außen ist, auch innen'.

[88] *Kyrios Jesus*, p.39, 'Diese Verknüpfung von ethischer Setzung und natürlichen Geschehen ist nur einer göttlichen Gestalt möglich.'

An important part of Lohmeyer's argument that Paul is quoting a hymn and that the words 'death of the cross' are an addition of Paul to the hymn is that the hymn says nothing about the religious effects of the servant's death. Lohmeyer notes two viewpoints in the New Testament. According to one, Christ's death needs the resurrection to vindicate it as the power and wisdom of God. According to the other, Christ's death is itself his glorification, his 'going to the Father'. Lohmeyer finds in the hymn of Philippians 2.5-11 a view of Christ's death closer to that of the Fourth Gospel than to that of Paul (p.45).

With the fourth stanza the language about Christ's exaltation is reached. Lohmeyer notes again that there is nothing in these words about resurrection or a return to a previous state or status. He seems to understand the exaltation in terms of the bestowing of the 'name above all names'. Indeed, he argues that the phrase 'name above all names' in the fourth stanza corresponds exactly to the phrase 'equal with God' in the first stanza. Christ, in receiving the name above all names, receives something that the divine form (*Gestalt*) did not previously possess (p.50).

The name is Kyrios, Lord. It denotes the totality of the divine reality: its form as well as in its being.[89] The name indicates the completeness of the divine reality. Lohmeyer notes that in later Judaism the phrase 'the name' assumes greater importance as a designation for God. He also notes a connection between 'the name' and 'the spirit'. In the hymn in I Timothy 3.16, Jesus is said to be 'justified in the spirit', something that happens to Jesus after his historical existence. In that passage from the Pastoral Epistles, Jesus is endowed

---

[89] *Kyrios Jesus*, p.50, 'Er [der Name] bezeichnet die Gesamtheit der göttlichen Wirklichkeit, ihre Gestalt wie ihr Sein'.

with the Spirit after his exaltation, so that through him the Spirit can be received by believers (p.55). The notion of 'the name' contains two things: the Exalted One is the mediation between God and the world. The one gifted with the Spirit is the mediation between God and the Christian community.

The central idea of the fifth stanza is that of all knees bowing at the 'name above all names'. In the present age, the world is subject to the devil. God's decree has resolved that every part of the world – heaven, earth and underworld – should be subject to the 'name above all names'. Jesus is to be Lord, not only of the Christian community, but of the world.

Lohmeyer has called the passage a psalm; but he admits that it lacks the usual features of the (Old Testament) psalms in the sense of a relationship between God and a believing individual or community (p.62). He replies that the question of the problems of believers is subsumed in the matter of the fate of the world, and the meaning of their destiny. The passage also lacks the usual features of apocalyptic literature, such as a heavenly interpreter, or mysterious symbols and numbers. In today's words, by which Lohmeyer presumably means his philosophical understanding of the world as derived from Hönigswald, the psalm is a poem wrestling with an intellectual problem in the form of a myth.[90] But the content of the myth, although drawn from Old Testament sources such as Daniel 7 and Isaiah 53, has been occasioned by the historical circumstance of the life and death of Jesus.

It is not surprising that this myth became part of the liturgy of the Early Church, with its dual hope in the presence of Christ in its worship and of his imminent return expressed in the

---

[90] *Kyrios Jesus*, p.63, 'Eine Ideendichtung in Form eines Mythos'.

words *Maranatha*. It is also no surprise that the myth was part of a process that led to the emergence of Christology.

There is, however, a conclusion of Lohmeyer about the poem which has been much criticised by later interpreters of the passage. Lohmeyer argues that the title 'Christ' which comes in the phrase 'Jesus Christ is Lord' cannot be deduced from the content of the myth, but must have been presupposed. If Christ is excluded as the one responsible for the act of obedient self-sacrifice, who was responsible? It is a 'he' who was in the form of God, a 'he' who was a Son of Man, or a 'he' who was exalted by God to be Lord of all. There are different forms of the one and the same revelation. But what is revealed? What is revealed is a divine law: *per ardua ad astra* or, through human humility to divine exaltation. This law is fundamental to the idea of creation and to its completion as an act of God. For religious faith, it is the certainty of the eschatological completion of God's creative work, grounded in the fact of the lordship of Christ. This completion of creation is not something that comes to it from outside; it is already implicit in the work of creation.

Lohmeyer's determined anti-metaphysical stance has brought him a lot of criticism. R. P. Martin has commented:

> In Lohmeyer's estimate it is not the worthiness of Christ that is honoured, but this law which is being exemplified...To start from an *a priori* philosophical conviction like this is hardly the best method of exegetical approach'.[91]

---

[91] R. P Martin, *Carmen Christi. Philippians ii.5-11 in Recent Interpretation and in the Setting of Early Christian Worship*, Cambridge: Cambridge University Press, 1967, p.234.

Ernst Käsemann is similarly critical.[92] Yet Martin repeatedly refers to Lohmeyer's insights, while Käsemann acknowledges that Lohmeyer's interpretation has an incomparable attraction. This raises the unanswerable question of how far Lohmeyer's profound insights were the fruit of Hönigswald's influence, and whether they would have occurred to him otherwise.

Whatever criticisms can be made against it, Lohmeyer's *Kyrios Jesus* was a watershed in the study of the Philippian hymn, but at the same time an integral part of the unique and distinctive path that he was beginning to mark out as a biblical scholar.

---

[92] E. Käsemann, 'Kritische Analyse von Phil. 2.5-11', *Zeitschrift für Theologie und Kirche* 47 (1950), pp.313-360.

CHAPTER EIGHT

The 'Kairos' Essay

In 1920 a working group was formed in Berlin called the Kairos Group. It was an expression of religious Socialism, and in the 1920s published a journal entitled, *Blätter für religiösen Sozialismus*. Among the theologians who belonged to the group were Günther Dehn (1882-1970), who was at that time a pastor in the Berlin working-class district of Moabit, and Karl Ludwig Schmidt (1891-1951), Professor of New Testament in Gießen (1921), Jena (1925) and Bonn (1929). The best-known theological participant was Paul Tillich, who, in 1926 and 1929, edited two volumes of essays on behalf of the Kairos Group.[93] To what extent Lohmeyer was an active member of the group I do not know,[94] but he contributed an essay to the second publication entitled, 'Kritische und Gestaltende Prinzipien im Neuen Testament' ('Critical and Formative Principles in the New Testament').[95] He was presumably attracted philosophically and theologically to the work of the group by its emphasis on eschatology – the notion of 'Kairos' as the decisive moment which called for ethical ideas and social formations appropriate to the decisive moment.[96]

In the event, Lohmeyer produced an essay that crystallised and summarised his thoughts on Jesus, Paul and John that

---

[93] W. Schlüssler, E. Sturm, *Paul Tillich, Leben-Werk-Wirkung*, Darmstadt: Wissenschaftliche Buchgesellschaft, 2007, pp.11-12.
[94] Köhn gives no information.
[95] In P. Tillich (ed.), *Protestantismus als Kritik und Gestaltung*, Darmstadt: Otto Reich Verlag, 1929, pp.41-69.
[96] See Schlüssler and Sturm, *Tillich*, p.11.

became the basis of his subsequent detailed work and (sadly) unfinished projects. It represented some of the ideas in his *Vom Begriff der religiösen Gemeinschaft*, but displayed a greater maturity and confidence than the earlier work. An exposition of it here will make it possible to move in later chapters straight to the commentaries on the 'Captivity Epistles' and the commentaries on Matthew and Mark.

In the opening essay of the collection, Tillich had seen in the notion of *grace* (*Gnade*) the distinctive Christian revelation that served as a criticism of society and a pointer to its ideal form. For Lohmeyer, the distinctive feature was *faith* (*Glaube*). On the other hand, faith was a trusting abandonment of the self into God's hands that lifted the believer into a realm removed from critique and the task of reshaping society. At the same time, faith brought the awareness that the world was God's handiwork and could not be exempt from God's will and working. Thus faith said both 'no' and 'yes' to the matters of critique and the reshaping of society. This 'no' and 'yes' kind of paradoxical reasoning was to play an important role in the essay.

The faith of Early Christianity measured everything that existed and occurred by one and the same standard, and that standard was faith itself. But in this case, what order could emerge from the chaos that faith showed the world to be? The answer is that faith became the measure and reality, the form and content of everything that was to be established. It owed nothing to anything exterior to it, but was the principle of its own existence. It was because of this that Early Christian faith was able to challenge and overcome the Ancient World in which it originated. It provoked new ways of how life should be lived and experienced. Augustine gave classical expression to these impulses; but the New Testament remained – and remains – the reservoir of the impulses that were generated by faith, and which retain their power.

The opening pages show Lohmeyer writing in his most allusive, suggestive, and almost mystical style. The challenge of the essay was how these visionary ideas could be worked out in practice.

Lohmeyer began with Judaism, because it was Judaism which most clearly challenged the standards of the Ancient World, and which offered, in the law bestowed upon the people by a gracious God, a pattern of how society could be shaped and how life could be lived. Unfortunately, the fact that the Jewish nation had become a religious community with no political power to hold it together had resulted in Judaism becoming the stage for bitter disputes between religious factions over the interpretation and practical observance of the God-given law. Jesus had to be understood in the context of these religious disputes. His message 'repent' implied that the people were no longer 'holy'. If he believed himself to be sent to the 'lost sheep of the house of Israel', this implied that all was not well with the flock. The positive part of his message was that the 'kingdom of God has drawn near'. Although the hope of the coming of God's kingdom was part of Israel's shared heritage, its coming was something that only God could bring about, and in announcing its immanence Jesus was speaking in the spirit of the Old Testament prophets. However, he differed from them, according to Lohmeyer, in one vital respect.

The prophets were people of their times, speaking to their time. The Kingdom of God transcends all time and times. It is an eternal 'now', which contains the meaning of the past and the future. Because of this, it concerns not only the Jewish people; it is universal. Further, by its nature, its message and

meaning are not tied to a particular time. It is eschatological –
lifted above present, past and future, yet disclosing the
meaning of the present, past and future. It gives form and
content to faith.

If it has a unique relationship to time, it also has a unique
relationship to human action, because the kingdom can only
be brought by God and not by human effort. This, according
to Lohmeyer, is why Jesus is critical of the piety of his day. No
fulfilling of the God-given law can bring the kingdom. This is
the meaning of the saying of Jesus that in order to enter the
kingdom one must become like a child. If it requires adults to
do what is not possible, this is because the kingdom is an
impossibility which alone makes the impossible possible.

This viewpoint affects how the teaching of Jesus is to be
understood. In the first place, his teaching is secondary to his
actions, in which the kingdom is manifested. His reply to John
the Baptist's question, 'Are you he that should come?' is to
heal the sick, the blind and the lame, and to appraise John of
these deeds. Only at the end come the words, 'The Gospel is
preached to the poor'. On the face of it, much of the teaching
of Jesus is based upon examples from everyday peasant life,
and appears to give straightforward instruction. To say this, is
to overlook the double- or deeper-sidedness of the teaching. If
Jesus teaches the possible, 'What you wish others to do to you,
so do to them', he also commands the impossible, 'Be perfect
as your heavenly Father is perfect', or says, 'If you have faith
and say to this mountain rise up and cast yourself into the sea
it will be done.'

> The kingdom proclaimed and actuated by Jesus is
> eschatological. It is above, yet bound to past, present and
> future. This Kingdom of God is thus a fundamental
> critique of everything that exists, because it tests all

realities against his own reality; but at the same time it is the only possible form, because its form is the basis and aim of all the historical formations.[97]

What applies to the kingdom also applies to Jesus, who is its witness and its guarantor. The kingdom is present in the life and work of Jesus, and is thus the fulfilment of all events and endeavours; it is the fullness of divine revelation. This, however, leads to a problem. The death of Jesus brings to an end the kingdom as embodied in his life and work. What form can it take after his death? This question is answered by Lohmeyer in the next two sections, respectively, on Paul and John.

Lohmeyer's section on Paul anticipates and succinctly summarises his later major work *Grundlagen Paulinischer Theologie (Basics of Pauline Theology)* (1929). Paul's major difficulty lies in the concept and existence of the Jewish Law. On the one hand it is God-given, and thus universal. It defines the Jewish people as the historical embodiment of God's ideal form of communal life for all peoples. At the same time, it is limited by being confined to one people. Also, because it is caught up in the vicissitudes of human history, it cannot always serve as God's ideal image for human life. A further difficulty arises because despite being God's law, it relies upon human obedience for its realisation. Thus, while it is a revelation from God, its dependence upon human obedience means that it cannot be the revelation of God in an absolute sense. Its dependence upon human fulfilment compromises its religious validity. It is, to quote Paul, 'holy, just and good' (Romans 7.12), yet it is limited in what it can achieve.

---

[97] Lohmeyer, 'Prinzipien', p.55, 'Dieses Reich Gottes bedeutet darum die grundsätzlich Kritik an allem Gegebenen, weil es all Wirklichkeiten an seinen eigenen Wirklichkeiten prüft, und ist zugleich die einzig mögliche Gestalt, weil diese seine Gestalt aller geschichtlichen Gestaltungen Grund und Ziel ist.'

This dilemma is solved for Paul, according to Lohmeyer, by the coming of Christ. He fulfilled the law, something that is affirmed by the Resurrection. This fulfilment shows him to be the divine Lord, who also lives a human life and suffers a human death. This makes him a mediator between God and humanity. It enables people who are living as part of the world of humanity to reject the world and live wholly for God. But how is this possible? The life of Christ, which fulfils the law, is lived in a segment of history. How can this affect individuals who do not belong to that segment? Paul proceeds along two lines, according to Lohmeyer.

First, the life of Christ is such that it bursts all historical barriers and in his obedience becomes a timeless demonstration of the sinful nakedness of the human race before God. Secondly, God provides a new miracle, namely, that of faith: 'Faith is the divine power which binds the individual to God and which endows him in this relationship with the righteousness of God.'[98] Faith, as understood in this way, is free of any social manifestation; but it is Paul's unique contribution, according to Lohmeyer, for faith to be linked to community. Faith affects the individual, but it also creates a community distinctively shaped by faith. The community is that of 'our Lord' and is 'his body'. One is reminded here of Hönigswald's account of the inter-subjectivity of the individual monads. The function of the community created by faith is to continue the work begun by Christ, which gives it its missionary mandate and character. But it is God who is at work within it. Lohmeyer cites I Corinthians 3.6:

I planted ... but God made it grow.

---

[98] 'Prinzipien', p.60, 'Glaube ist also die göttliche Macht, die den Einzelnen an Gott bindet und ihm in solcher Gebundenheit Gerechigkeit Gottes schenkt'.

The Early Christian community, like the Jewish community from which it grew, initially has two sides to it: its origins in what God has made possible, and its embodiment among fragile human beings and its existence in the world. It can be said to be a renewal of all that is found within Judaism, but with this difference. It witnesses to the eschatological end that has already become present in the life and work of Jesus. Its presence in the world is a critique of the world and its orders. It points beyond its own limitations to the possibilities that God has created through the work of faith.

If, for Lohmeyer, Paul is the man of action, John is the man of thought and contemplation. If, for Paul, the problem was that of the Jewish law, for John it was the problem of creation. How could it be that a world created by God had come under the domination of Satan? There is no attempt to answer that question. Instead, John sees in the coming of Christ into the world the culmination of a process begun long before in human history: 'The light shines in the darkness, and the darkness has not overcome it' (John 1.5). In Jesus the fullness of God's will for the world becomes present in the world: 'The Son is the pure revelation of the Father; the Father the pure revealer of the Son'.[99]

The coming of the Son into the world shows that the world, in its response to the Son, is a place of falsehood, darkness and error. The whole Gospel of John is dominated by the dualism of two worlds. It is almost possible to say (these are not Lohmeyer's exact words, but the idea is strongly implied, I would maintain) that the purpose of Christ's coming is to complete God's creative work; to establish a relationship of

---

[99] 'Prinzipien', p.64, 'Der Sohn ist die reine Offenbarung des Vaters, der Vater der reine Offenbarer des Sohnes'.

oneness between God and his creation. This is why the Word becomes flesh.

The notion of eschatology is never far from Lohmeyer's thought, and his section on John is no exception. Eschatology in John, according to Lohmeyer, is the continual struggle of eternal fulfilment striving towards eternal fulfilment. It is thus a striving to conform a dysfunctional world to God's ideal fulfilment that makes it God's world; and it becomes increasingly God's world, not by some natural process of growth and development, but by the overpowering divine forces immanent at work in it, and of which the coming of Christ is an instance.

Lohmeyer sees a close connection between this Johannine account of the significance of Jesus and the preaching of Jesus himself. Jesus is certain that he is part of the coming kingdom or rule of God that is now present, and is thus fulfilment and future hope and promise. This approach does, however, have implications for how the community of those who believe in Jesus is to function in the world. If, for Paul, the believing community has a divine mission to spread the Gospel, for John, according to Lohmeyer, its function is to embody God's love. It is in the action of love that God's power will be enabled to complete the work of creation, made possible in Christ.

CHAPTER NINE

The Commentaries on the 'Captivity Epistles'

In 1928 Lohmeyer published the first of his commentaries to appear in the Meyer series of commentaries which had been established by Heinrich August Wilhelm Meyer (1800-1873). It dealt with the Letter to the Philippians, and was soon followed by commentaries on Colossians and Philemon (1930), all three appearing together in one volume in 1930. Lohmeyer had, of course, published a commentary on the Book of Revelation in the *Handbuch zum Neuen Testament* series in 1926, (see chapter six).

In his new commentaries, especially that on Philippians, he continued to follow his highly personal and individualistic path as a New Testament scholar, advancing theories about the literary structure and the location of the writing of the books that have found almost no acceptance among later scholars, while at the same time producing many profound insights into the nature of Christian belief and practice. Indeed, to read these commentaries on Paul's letters (Lohmeyer held Paul to be the writer of Colossians) is to be immersed at times in profound meditation. Yet these are not the result of preaching or of pietistic platitudes. They are won from Lohmeyer's relentless attention to the minutiae of the Greek biblical text, informed by his philosophical grounding in the system of Hönigswald.

Philippians

That the letter to the Philippians is not a literary unity is the generally accepted view of modern New Testament scholarship.[100] Anyone reading the English text can note that chapter 2.19-29 ends with the personal details that usually conclude Paul's letters, and that chapter 3 begins abruptly and appears to deal with matters not previously mentioned in the letter. However, while acknowledging these facts, Lohmeyer defended the unity of the letter. He did so by maintaining something that has found no support among later scholars, namely, that the letter is characterised throughout by the idea of martyrdom.[101] His argument runs as follows.

Paul, writing in AD 58, is imprisoned in Caesarea. He expects the verdict to go against him and to be condemned to death. At the same time, the Christian community in Philippi has suffered harassment, and some of its leaders and members may be in prison. They, too, may be facing martyrdom, as Paul is. The purpose of the letter, therefore, is to encourage the Christians there to be united with each other, to be faithful to Christ, and to know that as Paul awaits martyrdom he is united with them in their sufferings under persecution. Further, Paul expounds the nature of martyrdom in the light of Christ's martyrdom. It is a work of grace (p.67), and completes the 'freedom of the children of God' (p.60). Further, it takes place in the context of a world that has been changed by Christ's self-abasement, which is his exaltation (pp.92-3).

---

[100] See F. Laub, 'Philipperbrief' in *Neues Bibel Lexikon*, vol. 4, pp.137-8.
[101] See P. Bonnard, *L'Épître de Saint Paul aux Philippiens* (Commentaire du Nouveau Testament X), Neuichâtel: Delachaux et Niestlé, 1950, p.9. 'La situation de l'Église de Philippes, au moment où l'apôtre lui écrit, elle non plus, ne peut-être complètement reconstituée. C'est ce qui à permis à Lohmeyer d'imaginer une Église dans le feu de la persécution, à laquelle l'apôtre enverrait une sorte de traité théologique sur le martyre'. Bonnard rejects this view.

This being so, Lohmeyer analyses the letter as follows:

A   Address and benediction (1.1-2)
B   Preface (1.3-11) Thanks (1.3-6),
    Personal (1.7-8), Prayer (1.9-11)
C   Main section (1.12 to 4.9):
I   Martyrdom of Paul (1.12-26)
II Martyrdom of the community (1.27 to 2.16)
III Assistance in martyrdom (2.17-30)
IV The dangers in martyrdom (3.1-21)
V   Final warnings in martyrdom (4.1-9)
D   Final word: financial help (4.18-20)
E   Greetings and benediction (4.21-23)

Lohmeyer addresses the difficulty that chapter 3 seems to deal with a quite different topic, namely, the danger of Judaising Christians, by suggesting, among other things, that whereas Judaism was a recognised and protected religion in the Roman empire, Christianity was not. Paul is warning Christians faced by persecution not to join or re-join the Synagogue in order to gain its protection.

Another problem that Lohmeyer has to face is Paul's assertion that he hopes shortly to make a visit to the church in Philippi (2.24, and see also 1.26). How is this possible if he thinks he is facing imminent martyrdom? Lohmeyer invokes the idea of 'eschatological completion' (*Vollendung*, pp.69-70). His life, and that of the Philippian church, is lived in the context of two 'endings': that of martyrdom, and that of the Parousia, Christ's coming again. In both cases Paul will be reunited with his correspondents. These ideas determine the sense of a speedy reunion, rather than Pauline travel plans following a possible release from captivity. While this may not sound convincing, it has to be noted that both passages (1.26 and 2.24) do not unambiguously indicate an imminent physical reunion.[102]

---

[102] See, for example, Bonnard, *Philippiens*, pp.31-2, 55-6.

The important thing about martyrdom in Paul's thought, according to Lohmeyer, is that it is not simply a noble expression of Christian obedience, in which the example of Christ is followed. To suppose this is to miss Paul's emphasis on his belief that Christ's self-abasement and thus his exaltation is an action of God which has destroyed the powers of evil, and has established God's lordship in the world in a new way. 'The action of God is the central point of the poem', that is, the poem in 2.5-11. The use of the word 'Father' in the phrase, 'Glory of God the Father' (2.11), indicates God's triumph. In order to wrest the world from Satanic power and return it to God, the divine 'form' undertakes the journey from heaven to earth. That he became Lord is the sign that the victory has been won. It is possible to say, on the basis of the word 'Father', that God and the world are now reconciled and are one.[103] Martyrdom is an action made possible by God in the new situation that God has created. It is a witness to Christ; but it is not an obligation but a form of existence; not a requirement but a privilege.[104]

Lohmeyer's emphasis on the initiative of God, and how this affects everything, can be seen especially in his treatment of 2.12-13, 'Work out your own salvation ... for God is at work in you'. It occurs in the section immediately following the 'Christ poem' in what is understood by Lohmeyer as a practical commentary on the hymn (p.99). 'Salvation' in this passage means 'eschatological completion' and it has come close to each Christian in Philippi to achieve (work out) the prospect

---

[103] Lohmeyer, *Philipperbrief*, p.98, 'Um die Welt den satanischen Mächten zu entreißen und Gott wieder zuzuführen, trat die göttliche Gestalt den Gang vom Himmel zur Erde an. Dass sie Kurios wurde, ist das Zeichen, dass der Sieg errungen ist. Darum kann in dem Worte "Vater" davon gesprochen werden, dass jetzt Gott und die Welt "versöhnt" und eines sind'.
[104] *Philipperbrief*, p.84, '"Für Christus", reden ... nicht von einem Sollen, sondern von einem Sein, nicht von einer Forderung, sondern von einer Begnadung'.

of martyrdom, which is the situation in which the community lives. But the passage also makes clear that any believing action is also the action of God. It does not speak of a kind of divine and human mutual co-operation. 'To act' means to be acted upon by God; he is the sole ground that makes the action of the individual possible and real.[105]

The prospect of martyrdom is also illuminated in Philippians, according to Lohmeyer, by Paul's eschatological emphases. Commenting on 1.5-6, 'Thankful for your partnership in the Gospel from the first day until now', and 'I am sure that he who began a good work in you will bring it to completion on the day of Jesus Christ', Lohmeyer writes about the time-points that come in the passage: 'the first day', 'now', and 'the day of Jesus Christ'. These are not normal points on a timescale stretching from the past to the future via the present. 'The first day' was not the beginning of a learning process. It was the point at which faith became a reality. The 'now' is not a point in time to be followed by a tomorrow and a future. It will be fulfilled by 'the day of Jesus Christ', which means that it is cut off from usual time, and gains its significance from something that reveals and will reveal ultimate truth and value. In the 'now' the believer experiences what is eternal and will be consummated in 'the day of Jesus Christ'. Lohmeyer compares it to the first day of the Genesis creation narrative. The three time references: 'first day', 'now', and 'day of Jesus Christ', together make an unbroken ring. It is difficult not to think of Stefan George at this point.

A similar point is made in different terms in the introduction to 1.27-2.16. The community in Philippi is being persecuted, and faces the likelihood of the completion of faith from two

---

[105] *Philipperbrief*, p.103, 'Wirken heißt von Gott gewirkt sein; er ist der einzige Grund, der das Wirken des Einzelnen möglich und wirklich macht'.

angles: either martyrdom and death or the Parousia, the return of Christ. Both possibilities are centred in the Lord. Present, past and future are bound together by faith, suffering and consummation.

Another notable passage occurs in Lohmeyer's exposition of Paul's account of his passage from Judaism to faith in Christ in 3.9. Paul speaks of having a righteousness based not on law, but which is through faith in Christ. Lohmeyer indicates what he believes had become Paul's central problem, that the divine law demanded action without creating the possibility that it could be carried out. Paul thus posits an alternative righteousness, which is God's righteousness. It is made possible by three moments: first, the overcoming of the world by God in the suffering and death of Christ. The second is the miracle of faith. This is something that God makes happen to people, and is not merely a human experience. A human experience makes individuals aware of themselves, but the form of coming to faith extinguishes what is particular to an individual. It relates to Christ and involves the overcoming of the opposition between God and the world. It bestows faith and righteousness. It can be described by the term 'being experienced' (*Erlebtwerden*), rather than experiencing (pp.137-138). The faith that is engendered is eschatological. It is a penultimate (*Vorletztes*) that is determined by and waits in hope for its final completion.

Terminology derived from Hönigswald can also be found in the commentary. Philippians 2.2 reads: '[Have] the same love, being in full accord and of one mind'. Lohmeyer explains that the individual (the 'I') from the Christian point of view is defined in relation to God by means of the gift of faith. In this way it is bound together with other 'I's, the monadic constitution of the 'I' is swallowed up in the unity of faith and love made possible by God. The individuality of the historical 'I' is abolished in the equality of the religious souls (p.86).

Colossians

Whether or not Paul wrote the letter to the church of Colossae is a matter of dispute among New Testament scholars. There is also the matter of its close relationship to the Letter to the Ephesians, the Pauline authorship of which is more strongly questioned. Lohmeyer's intention to write on Ephesians gave way to his work on Mark and later, Matthew.[106] But he made an interesting, Hönigswald-type comment on the relationship between Colossians and Ephesians, something that would also affect his work on Matthew. This comment was to the effect that whatever the literary relationship between these individual writings might be, each had to be regarded as a work in its own right, and had to be commented on in this light.[107] The same point would affect his commentary on Matthew, where he treated passages that were clearly dependent upon Mark as nevertheless pieces in their own right. The connection with the thought of Hönigswald is the theory of the monad, and that each monad is a unique entity, however much it may be possible to identify the individual components of which it is made up.

In his introduction to the commentary on Colossians, Lohmeyer set out fully the factors that had led to the questioning of its Pauline authorship since 1838. These included not only the number of Greek words that were unique to the book, but also the way in which the words were put together, which made their translation almost impossible at times. Lohmeyer attributed some of this difficulty to Paul's use of traditional

---

[106] See *Philipperbrief*, preface, dated September 1929.
[107] E. Lohmeyer, *Der Brief an die Kolosser*, p.9, note 2.

phrases that owed their structure to Semitic or Aramaic thought forms. For his own part, Lohmeyer did not doubt Pauline authorship. The letter was probably composed during Paul's imprisonment in Caesarea in the summer of AD58, before the composition of Philippians during the late summer of the same year. At the time of writing, his trial had not yet taken place, whereas when he wrote Philippians it had taken place and Paul strongly sensed a verdict against him and the likely prospect of martyrdom. However, the possibility of martyrdom was real to him when he wrote Colossians, although it played a much less significant part in that letter compared with Philippians.

One of the main purposes of Colossians was to oppose the 'Colossian philosophy'. Lohmeyer identified this as a complex amalgam of Hellenistic and Jewish speculations within a framework drawn from Iranian religion. At its centre was the idea of the elemental spirits of the world, defined as angelic powers, which held together the disparate parts of the world and reflected dimly something of the nature of God. Access by the human soul to God was by way of these elemental spirits.

One of the characteristic features of Lohmeyer's commentaries was the considerable amount of space that he devoted to minute analysis of the opening greetings of the letters and the prayers that followed. 'Prayer is to faith what breath is to life; faith and prayer is one and the same', he wrote.[108] He followed this up with a detailed treatment of thanksgiving (*Dank*), which played a more important role in Colossians than in any other Pauline letter. The 'Colossian philosophy' endangered the basis of all that God had done through Christ. To give

---

[108] *Kolosserbrief*, p.32, 'Das Gebet ist dem Glauben, was das Atem dem Leben ist; glauben und beten ist eins und dasselbe'.

thanks for what God had done was the only possible way of being bound to God:

> Whoever does not give thanks remains forever distant from God. Whoever gives thanks knows what he himself and everything else owes to God.[109]

To be a community of faith means to be the bearers of thanksgiving.

In treating the first part of chapter 1, Lohmeyer took verses 13-20 to be a unity, in which he detected two main parts, each with three lines followed by seven lines. The unit was divided as follows:

> He has delivered us from the dominion of darkness
> And transferred us to the kingdom of his beloved Son
> In whom we have the redemption, the forgiveness of sins.
> He is the image of the invisible God
> The first-born of all creation:
> For in him all things were created,
> In heaven and earth,
> Visible and invisible,
> Whether thrones or dominions,
> Or principalities or authorities.
> All things were created through him and for him.
> He is before all things
> And in him all things hold together.
> He is the head of the body, the church;
> He is the beginning, the first-born from the dead,
> That in everything he might be pre-eminent.
> For in him all the fullness of God was pleased to dwell,
> And through him to reconcile to himself all things,
> Making peace by the blood of his cross
> [Through him][110] on earth or in heaven.

---

[109] *Kolosserbrief*, p.38, 'Wer nicht dankt, bleibt Gott immer fern; wer aber dankt, weiß ihm sich selbst und alles schuldig'.

[110] Lohmeyer read *di autou* with many ancient authorities.

This division enabled Lohmeyer to argue that the weight of the passage was to be found in Christ, and that the two units taken together stressed Christ's relationship to the world: in creation (first unit) and salvation (second unit). This led, further, to the argument that the implied background to the whole passage was the Jewish Day of Atonement which, in Jewish tradition, was not only a day of forgiveness but was also linked to creation, in that the forgiveness effected on the Day of Atonement was a kind of re-creation of the world. Lohmeyer cited what he admitted was the late (in fact, ninth-century AD) tractate *Pesiqta Rabbati* as the clearest statement of this tradition. At the creation, God had separated light from darkness and what was above from what was beneath, in order to establish peace between these opposites on the Day of Atonement.

On the basis of a consideration of this background a clear idea of Paul's meaning in this passage could be gained. In place of the Day of Atonement was the work of Christ. Further, the cosmic function of Christ's work in the passage pointed to the eschatological figure of the Son of Man, who is sometimes seen in Jewish tradition as the first Adam, as Lord of all that is created. The Son of Man in Jewish apocalyptic tradition destroys the power of Satan and the demons and thus overcomes the cosmic dualism that characterises the world. This is God's doing. The phrase 'for in him', i.e., Christ, is important here. The whole piece of explanation is a fine example of Lohmeyer's work as a commentator.

However, if this is a fine example of Lohmeyer at his clearest, what follows, the detailed exegesis of 1.13-20 shows the more formidable and difficult side of Lohmeyer. Densely packed passages explore the possible Jewish and Hellenistic backgrounds to the language used. Implicit paradoxes are identified and developed in various directions. The statement 'that in him all things were created' is found to be particularly difficult, as it is the problem of how the world can have come into being in him (Christ) when he is the one through whose death the world has been reconciled. While Paul might have seen a resolution in terms of faith, Lohmeyer points out that Paul does not mention faith at this point. Lohmeyer finds a solution partly in the 'Colossian philosophy' and its belief in the elements that have constituted the world. Faith plays its part in identifying Christ and the elements to which he is superior. All this speculation occurs at the level of the metaphysical and not at the level of the 'I''s relatedness. The 'I' relatedness occurs in 1.21-23, when Paul addresses the community of believers, especially in the words 'and you, who were estranged ... he has now reconciled'.

The word 'now' is an important one for Lohmeyer, and he gives it a full treatment. It is not a mere point in the stream of passing time. It is rather a 'now' which, in the light of God's action, indicates something that is always present. The 'now' reaches back from the day on which God effected reconciliation through him (Christ), and stretches forward to the day when it will be completed with the Parousia, the coming of Christ. The 'now' also designates the believers in Colossae as those who have been reconciled. It is correct to connect the 'now' with the day on which Christ's reconciling work became the experience of the Colossian believers; but it is more than that. Here we see Lohmeyer's philosophical theological views expanding the sense of the text beyond its immediate context, something typical of his method and approach.

Another good example of this is Lohmeyer's handling of the phrase 'in him ([Christ] the whole fullness of deity dwells bodily'. Lohmeyer notes that the Greek word rendered 'deity' (*theotês*) is found neither in the Greek of the Old Testament nor elsewhere in the New Testament. This indicates that it comes from Greek thought and language, most likely from the 'Colossian philosophy'. The word 'fullness' suggests multiplicity, and is best understood in connection with a reference to the 'elemental spirits' in the previous verse. In fact, the phrase 'fullness of deity' as applied to Christ is not appropriate. The Christ who became man was not characterised by fullness, but by poverty. He had only received fullness after he became Lord through his resurrection. Thus Lohmeyer was able to contrast the philosophy of being of the 'Colossian philosophy' with the philosophy of divine action on the part of God's work in Christ, of which the latter led to the experience of being forgiven and reconciled. Through Christ's action, the world was delivered from the shadowy rule of the elemental spirits into the possibility and reality of believing existence.

This had the practical implication that rules about fasting and religious observances could be ignored or had at any rate ceased to be matters of disagreement. They were merely shadows of what had come to light in Christ. To observe them was to deny the freedom that Christ had given them (2.16-23). On the other hand, the believing community, living between the times – that of the first and second coming of Christ – needed guidelines by which to live, and these were provided in 3.18 to 4.1. These are usually called 'household codes' in the standard commentaries and, although it is not universally accepted that their origins lie in Greek Stoic teachings, the majority view tends to lean in this direction.[111]

---

[111] See the Excursus 'Die Haustafeln' in J. Gnilka, *Der Kolosserbrief* (Herders Theologischer Kommentar zum Neuen Testament), Freiburg: Herder Verlag, 2002, pp.205-216.

Lohmeyer argues that Paul was quoting selectively from Jewish diaspora codes of behaviour. The words were therefore mostly not his own, but the choice was his, determined by what he felt was essential for a community whose life was to be lived for the glory of God. The fact that women, together with children and slaves, are mentioned first was not accidental. Although the sentiments expressed reflected traditional Jewish views of the relationship of wives and their husbands, women were mentioned first so that it was clear that they were not second-class members of the believing community. The words addressed to slaves were influenced by Paul's belief that the notion of slavery to God best expressed the vocation and work of Christian apostles.

There is no need to comment further on Lohmeyer on Colossians, nor on the treatment of Philemon, which followed the widely, but not universally accepted, view that Onesimus was a runaway slave who was returning at Paul's behest to his master Philemon, although he would have preferred to remain with Paul as his helper.

Looking back over the commentaries it is impossible not to be impressed by the vast amount of work that they represent, all in all some 385 pages of closely-printed text, with many passages using smaller type for technical discussions. The amount of detail on textual-critical points, references to Jewish and Hellenistic background sources, not to mention secondary literature, the citing of which is relevant and judicious and not a display of knowledge for its own sake, is considerable; but above all what is most impressive, as earlier mentioned, is Lohmeyer's relentless interrogation of the minutiae of the Greek text at literary-aesthetic, grammatical and philosophical levels. As also mentioned earlier, without trying to preach or be deliberately didactic, Lohmeyer was able to make many observations about the life of faith that make reading the commentaries, for all their formidable language, at times inspiring and uplifting. Such insights surely cannot have been without connection to his own life and practice of faith.

CHAPTER TEN

The Breslau Rectoral Address

On 3 November 1930, Lohmeyer was inducted into the position of Rector of the University of Breslau. Although this position lasted for only one year, it meant considerable disruption to his normal routine of teaching, research and writing. The nearest equivalent position in a British University to that of a Rector in a German University is the position of Vice-Chancellor.

The biography by Andreas Köhn is especially valuable at this point because, drawing on the correspondence between Lohmeyer and the publishing firm of Vandenhoeck & Ruprecht, he is able to supply many personal details about Lohmeyer's life at that time. We learn, for example, that Lohmeyer was not particularly well between December 1929 and February 1930, and that this had affected his scholarly work. He had also served as the Dean of the Theological Faculty in 1930, and anticipated that his duties as Rector of the university would further disrupt his research and writing.[112]

Köhn also provides a valuable background sketch of the political situation that obtained in Germany at the beginning of Lohmeyer's period as Rector. This can be supplemented by the exhaustive treatment in Scholder's *The Churches and the Third Reich*.[113] According to Scholder, the question of German

[112] Köhn, *Lohmeyer*, p.53.
[113] K. Scholder, *Die Kirchen und das Dritte Reich. I Vorgeschichte und Zeit der Illusion 1918-1934*, Munich: Prophäen Taschenbuch, 2004.

national identity after the defeat of Germany in the First World War was particularly acute because, unlike the Roman Catholic Church, the Lutheran churches felt themselves to be especially 'German'. Younger theologians concerned themselves with the notion of people (*das Volk*), and the German people in particular, and the theological and historical implication of these notions. Theologians such as Emanuel Hirsch embraced ideas of the relationship between the Lutheran churches and the German people that would make them ready sympathisers with the Hitler movement and its anti-Semitism. It was possible to see the renewal of Germany as an opportunity for the Lutheran churches to further their mission to the German people.

Against the background of a new consciousness of being German and of rising anti-Semitism, Lohmeyer's address as Rector was remarkable for its content. As will be seen, it devoted a good deal of its space to the contribution that Ancient Israel and Judaism had made to his central theme of faith and history. Also, Lohmeyer was not afraid, in an academic address, to end by quoting John 1.14, 'The Word became flesh'.

There was one notable absentee from among Lohmeyer's hearers. Richard Hönigswald had left Breslau for Munich in 1930. Lohmeyer referred to him indirectly in his address as Rector as 'one of our colleagues who has left us this year',[114] and credited him with having shown the special meaning of 'beginning' in connection with the Israelite view of history. Hönigswald's departure from Breslau meant that correspondence between him and Lohmeyer intensified, and

---

[114] E. Lohmeyer, *Glaube und Geschichte in vorderorientalischen Religionen. Rede gehalten bei der Einführung in das Rektorat am 3. November 1930*, Breslauer Universitätsreden Heft 6, Breslau: Ferdinand Hirt, 1931, p.18.

Hönigswald wrote on 25 January 1931 to congratulate Lohmeyer on his address as Rector, which he and his family had read with great appreciation.[115]

Lohmeyer began by acknowledging that a university was a place of learning that embraced many disciplines. But did they have anything in common? Was there an underlying unity? His answer was that, ultimately, scholarly and scientific research was concerned with our existence as human beings. This, in turn, led to the question of faith and history, which was to be the subject of his address as Rector.

So far, 'faith' was left undefined. Lohmeyer began with ancient Babylon, in which he included Sumerian thought. Here, he argued, it was believed that history was determined by fate, by what was decreed by the gods. This meant that there was no distinction between history and faith. No-one questioned why things happened as they did. Also, the king was the visible representative and embodiment of the god, an intermediary between heaven and earth. Also important was the idea that the king's function was to use his power to establish and maintain order, an order that was willed by heaven.

This essentially harmonious view of reality was disturbed by the Iranian prophet of the eighth and seventh centuries BC, Zoroaster. According to him, so Lohmeyer, life was not determined by fate, but was to be lived in the pursuit of what was good, involving a continual struggle to overcome what was evil. Behind observable reality was a struggle between two cosmic principles of good and evil, later to be called Ormazd and Ahriman. Two kingdoms were in conflict, and humans had to choose to which to give allegiance. Lohmeyer

---

[115] W. Otto (ed.), *Aus der Einsamkeit – Briefe einer Freundschaft. Richard Hönigswald an Ernst Lohmeyer*, Würzburg: Königshausen und Neumann, 1999, pp.42-3.

saw in the teaching of Zoroaster something that would receive classic Christian expression in Augustine's work, *The City of God*.[116]

Although the Persian King Darius made Zoroastrianism the state religion, the prophet addressed himself to nomadic tribes, to whom his view of the equality of humans under their moral task was appealing. His views tended towards the creation of a 'church', that is, a community bound by faith, and belief, even though this was in the context of a state. The existence of the 'church' within the state led to new thinking. Although the state was predominant, the king became the servant of what was believed by the 'church'. The enemies of the state became the opponents of the faith affirmed by the 'church'. How history was viewed was also affected. It came to be seen as the interplay of divine and anti-divine laws.[117] The idea of divine power became a matter of faith on the part of believers. The world of metaphysical beliefs began to be created by human thinkers, and led to an eschatological idea of an 'end' of history that would make sense of the course of history.

From Zoroastrian religion Lohmeyer moved to that of Ancient Israel: 'Scarcely has any other religion so tirelessly wrestled with the problem of faith and history as this (i.e. Israelite religion)'.[118] The fact that it found no answer to the question was its most profound thought. But also central to the contribution was the idea of the *people*,[119] and of the existence or non-existence of a people in the flux of history.

---

[116] Lohmeyer, *Glaube und Geschichte*, p.12.
[117] *Glaube und Geschichte*, p.15, 'Geschichte ist das ewige Widerspiel menschlicher Kräfte, die unter einem göttlichen oder auch widergöttlichen Gesetze stehen'.
[118] *Glaube und Geschichte*, p.16, 'Kaum eine Religion hat so unablässig um das Problem von Glaube und Geschichte gerungen wie diese'.
[119] *Glaube und Geschichte*, p.16, 'der Gedanke des Volkes'.

With these words Lohmeyer was deliberately entering a minefield. In her important study, *The Old Testament and the National Question,* Cornelia Weber has traced the idea of the 'people' in German thought from its roots in the eighteenth and nineteenth centuries to the situation in post-World War II Germany and beyond.[120] The idea of a 'people' had assumed racist overtones with the conviction that the German people was a superior people because, among other things, of its achievements in such things as philosophy and the arts, not to mention the Reformation inaugurated by Martin Luther. The defeat of Germany in the First World War was very difficult to come to terms with, and the Weimar Republic was hated in many quarters because it had resulted from that defeat. The idea of the German people became a central term in the mind-set of the anti-democratic and anti-Weimar Republic forces that Hitler would come to spearhead. Anti-Semitism was part and parcel of this mind-set. The Jews living in Germany were regarded as an alien element among the German people. It was bold for Lohmeyer to claim that it was the Israelite religion that had developed the idea of a 'people', and that in doing so had made a decisive and lasting contribution to the question of the relationship between faith and history.

Lohmeyer posed the question, 'What is this people?' and answered it as follows. It was, first, a small buffer state among the great empires of the ancient world. It was also a tribal society cherishing the traditions of its ancestors; but, tied as it

---

[120] C. Weber, *Altes Testament und völkische Frage* (Forschungen zum Alten Testament 28), Tübingen: Mohr Siebeck, 2000. The subtitle reads *Der biblische Volksbegriff in der alttestamentlichen Wissenschaft der nationalsozialistischen Zeit, dargestellt am Beispiel von Johannes Hempel (1891-1964).* (The biblical idea of the 'people' in the Old Testament scholarship of the National Socialist period, examined from the example of Johannes Hempel (1891-1964). Hempel was professor in Göttingen (1928-37) and Berlin (1937-40) and a military Chaplain (1940-46). He was deprived of his chair because of his support for the National Socialist régime, and served as a Pastor in Salzgitter (1949-1957). In retirement he was made an emeritus professor in Göttingen (1958-1964).

was emotionally to its own small land, it had spread or been dispersed from this land. It was a linguistic community with a common language and ritual traditions. Above all, it was also a faith community, believing that its God had worked through its history over the centuries. It owed something to the Zoroastrian insight for the belief that its task was to take part in the unending struggle between good and evil. Its unique contribution, however, and here Lohmeyer paid indirect tribute to his former colleague Hönigswald, was its view of time. Its view of 'beginning' meant that everything that happened was seen to stand under the thought of an unconditional norm, which made sense of it. The timelessness of this norm pulls the active 'I' from the flow of time.[121] It is 'now', in which the unconditional demands of order are fulfilled. In such a 'beginning' God created the heavens and the earth, and the flux of human actions can be described as a carpet into which God's eternal thoughts are woven.

Lohmeyer attributed the illustration of the carpet to Augustine and Goethe, and Goethe certainly seems to have used the idea of a carpet in connection with his collection of poems, *West-östlicher Divan*.[122] It is noteworthy, however, that in 1900 Stefan George had published a collection of poems entitled *Der Teppich des Lebens* (*The Carpet of Life*) and it would be surprising if this was not also at the back of Lohmeyer's mind. Further, Gundolf, in his book on George, had made some interesting observations at the end of his chapter in *The Carpet of Life*. The final poem in the collection is entitled 'Der Schleier' ('The Veil') and Gundolf says that the poem expresses the 'prime' insight of every seer: that space and time with their various contents are but glimmers of that eternal present or

---

[121] *Glaube und Geschichte*, 'Die Zeitlosigkeit dieser Norm reißt das handelnde Ich aus dem Fluß der Zeit'.
[122] See Morwitz, *Kommentar zu George*, p.157.

timeless being that is experienced by the privileged 'I' as God, or the world, or life'.[123] A few lines earlier Gundolf had also written of the eternity of the here and now in the idea of the perceiving spirit.[124] Lohmeyer went on to cite von Ranke's famous dictum that 'every epoch is directly related to God'.[125]

The unique contribution of Ancient Israel was to bind faith and history together in a new way through the concept of a people in a special relationship to God. Yet this was not meant to be exclusive; God was the God of all nations, because he was the God of one people. From this 'antinomy', as he called it, Lohmeyer claimed that the notion of a Messiah had arisen. This idea brought into a unity the scattered moments of history as a God-directed process, a community that believed this to be so, the inter-relationship between believing individuals and the community from which they drew their faith, and a tension between one people and all nations:

> In the idea of the Messiah and his community, the mediating point (*Mittel*) is given that eternally and ultimately unites history to God and God to history. This one and true mediator (*Mittler*) between heaven and earth creates the believing community and grounds himself in it, which has come into being only through him. In limitless freedom from every living thing, because of his unconditional dependence upon God, and in limitless self-giving to every living thing because of his unconditional unity with God, this 'I' is the true unity of faith and history, which is always given, and given up.[126]

---

[123] Gundolf, *George*, p.192, 'Die Ureinsicht jedes Sehers: dass Raum und Zeit mit sämtlichen Inhalten nur Scheine des ewigen oder gegenwärtigen oder zeitlosen Wesens sind, das als Gott oder Welt oder Leben vom begnadeten Ich wahrgenommen ... wird'.

[124] Gundolf, *George*, 'Die Ewigkeit des Jetzt und Hier im ideensichtigen Geist'.

[125] L. von Ranke, *Über die Epochen der neuen Geschichte. Vorträge dem Könige Maximilian II von Bayern*, Historische-kritische Ausgabe, ed. T. Schedig, Munich: H. Bentung, 1971, p.60, 'jede Epoche steht unmittelbar zu Gott'.

[126] *Glaube und Geschichte*, p.25, 'So ist in dem Gedanken des Messias und seiner Gemeinschaft die Mitte gegeben, welche die Geschichte an Gott und Gott an

This long quotation gives a good example of the complexity of Lohmeyer's language and thought at this point. It also creates the suspicion that Lohmeyer's description of the notion of the Messiah owed less to ancient Jewish ideas as recorded in their texts, and more to Lohmeyer's philosophy as derived from Hönigswald.

Lohmeyer's closing words saw in the notion of the Messiah a ring, a term used by Stefan George and prominent in the commentary on Revelation, which bound together beginning and ending in a meaningful whole. He quoted the following lines of poetry from Goethe:

> With blessed hearts and pious hands
> The moving flood forms itself
> Gloriously into a crystal ball.[127]

He continued with poetically expressed sentences about the distance and nearness in terms of which faith saw divinely ordered history; how eschatological completion set history free from its inexorable flow and gave it a sense that could be grasped by faith; how it became what it always was, and what it would become.

'We stand on the threshold of Early Christianity' were the opening words of the final paragraph. All that had gone

---

die Geschichte ewig und endgültig bindet. Dieser eine und wahre Mittler zwischen Himmel und Erde schafft die gläubige Gemeinschaft, durch die er selber ist, und gründet sich in ihr, die nur durch ihn wird. Also in grenzenloser Freiheit von allen Lebendigen weil in unbedingter Abhängigkeit von Gott, und in grenzenloser Hingabe an alles Lebendigen, weil in unbedingter Einheit mit Gott, ist dieser Ich die wahrhafte Einheit von Glaube und Geschichte, die immer gegeben und immer aufgegeben ... ist'.

[127] 'Seligem Herzen, frommen Händen/Ballt sich die bewegte Flut/Herrlich zu kristalner Kugel.' J. W. von Goethe, 'Legende', lines 9-11 in 'Paria'. See Birus, H., K. Eibl (eds.), 'Gedichte, West-Östlicher Divan', in F. Apel *et al.* (eds.), *Goethe Werke Jubiläumsausgabe*, vol. 1, Darmstadt: Wissenshaftliche Buchgesellschaft, 1998, p.205.

before in the address was summed up from an Early Christian perspective in words that perfectly expressed the relationship between faith and history:

> The Word was made flesh
> And dwelt among us,
> And we beheld his Glory.

University of Wrocław (Breslau): The main administrative building (left), and the ornate doors leading to the historic festive hall (below)

University of Greifswald (below): The new building on Rubenowplatz, into which the Theological Faculty moved in 2000, has been renamed 'Ernst Lohmeyer House'

Glasegrund (above), the tiny hamlet where Lohmeyer and his family had a country retreat

CHAPTER ELEVEN

John the Baptist

However much Lohmeyer's duties as Rector of the University of Breslau may have interfered with his scholarly work, it does not seem to have curtailed it. In 1932 there appeared the first, and only, volume of the projected multi-volume series on Early Christianity that was meant to supplement Lohmeyer's commentaries on the Gospels. The plan of the series was as follows:

I   John the Baptist
II   Jesus
III   The Early Church
IV   Paul
V   John the Evangelist
VI   The Post-Apostolic Period
VII   Early Christianity in the History of the Orient

The volume on John the Baptist, 196 pages long, was divided into three sections: tradition, message, presuppositions; but there was an important introduction, in which Lohmeyer described the historical method that he proposed to follow.[128] He had already outlined this in his earlier *Soziale Fragen* (see above p.52), but it is worth reviewing it again, because his treatment of John the Baptist put it into practice in matters concerning the literary criticism of the Gospels, and it would serve as the assumption behind his commentaries on Mark and Matthew.

---

[128] E. Lohmeyer, *Das Urchristentum. 1. Buch. Johannes der Täufer*, Göttingen: Vandenhoeck & Ruprecht, 1932.

Lohmeyer was acutely aware of two problems in using the New Testament, and the Gospels in particular, to reconstruct history. First, its history concerned what God was believed to have done. Did this fatally compromise it from a secular historical point of view? Secondly, there was the problem of the part and the whole. Should gospel historical scholarship begin by scrutinising narratives in order to ascertain what was 'authentic' and what was not, and then build up a picture from what was deemed to be 'authentic'; or should it attempt to gain some overall picture from the sources taken as a whole, and then judge the individual narratives from that perspective? Obviously, there is no clear answer to either of these questions, and New Testament experts have been divided in their responses to them. Also, it is inevitable that some kind of circularity cannot be avoided, especially in the relationship of the part to the whole.

Lohmeyer's response was as follows. On the first question, while Paul had asserted as historical facts that 'Christ died for our sins according to the scriptures, was buried, and did the third day rise again, according to the scriptures' (I Corinthians 15.3-4), Jesus, as recorded in the Synoptic Gospels, appeared to be quite different from what was preached about him. His message concerned the Kingdom of God and was intelligible only within the context of contemporary Judaism. His mission and that of John the Baptist had to be assessed as having given rise to the Early Christianity that was preached and believed, and a credible historical basis for this had to be established.

With regard to the question of the parts and the whole, Lohmeyer came down on the side of working from the whole to the parts. He frequently took issue with Bultmann's *History of the Synoptic Tradition*, where Bultmann looked for reasons why and how the Early Church attributed to John the Baptist and Jesus sayings that they could not have said.[129] He also drew attention to the fact that it was difficult in Goethe's *West-östlicher Divan* collection to know which poems were by Goethe and which by Marianne von Willmer, whom Goethe had met in Frankfurt in 1814, and who had contributed to the collection.[130] At the same time, Lohmeyer did not accept that everything said in the Gospels about John was undoubtedly authentic. With Martin Dibelius and Bultmann, he regarded the saying, 'He that is least in the kingdom of God is greater than he' (Matthew 11.11), as a piece of Early Church polemic against the claims of the disciples of John.[131]

This section in Matthew 11.7-18 is from the 'sayings source', as Lohmeyer called it, and gave important information about the person of John, as opposed to the Marcan picture, that presented John merely as a 'forerunner'. Matthew described Jesus as connecting John with the prophecy of Malachi 3.1, 'Behold, I send my messenger before thy face', and as seeing in John both a prophet and more than prophet. It also linked John closely with Jesus (Matthew 11.18-19). John had been despised for his asceticism; Jesus, by contrast, was accused of being a glutton and a drunkard. Another significant passage was that in which Jesus asked his opponents whether John's baptism was from heaven, that is, from God (Mark 11.29-30 and parallels).

Lohmeyer did not shrink from turning to John's Gospel for information about John the Baptist. This Gospel's opening chapter significantly modified the picture given in the

---

[129] For example, *Das Urchristentum*, p.18, note 2.
[130] *Das Urchristentum*, p.8, note 1. See B. Hamacher, *Johann Wolfgang von Goethe. Entwürfe eines Lebens*, Darmstadt Wissenschaftliche Buch-gesellschaft, 2010, p.203; H. Birus, K. Eibl (eds.), 'Gedichte, West-Östlicher Divan' in F. Apel *et al.* (eds.), *Goethe Werke Jubiläumsausgabe*, vol. 1, Darmstadt: Wissen-schaftliche Buchgesellschaft, 1998, pp.111-112.
[131] *Das Urchristentum*, p.19, note 1.

Synoptic Gospels. The first disciples met Jesus not in Galilee but in 'Bethany beyond the Jordan' (John 1.28); and John's activity is later located at 'Aenon, near Salim' (John 3.23), which Lohmeyer located in the region of Samaria. This was evidence that John's activity was not confined to the wilderness of Judaea. There was also the evidence in Acts 18.24 to 19.7 that there were former followers of John in Ephesus during the early years of Christianity.

Lohmeyer's survey did not end with the New Testament, but extended through Josephus and the testimony of the Early Church Fathers, including the Pseudo-Clementines and their account of Dositheus of Samaria, said to be a disciple of John the Baptist.

In a closing section to the first part of the book, Lohmeyer surveyed what had preceded it. He admitted that, in the case of the sources other than the New Testament, the sources were too opaque and uncertain, but they posed the question of why the impact of John the Baptist should have been such as to generate these traditions. The same could be said of John's Gospel, whose different picture of the Baptist compared with that of the Synoptics was often rejected as unhistorical and due to the theology of the Fourth Gospel; but to say this did not explain why this theology, in presenting the work of Jesus, paid the attention that it did to the work of John the Baptist.[132]

There were two more parts of the book to come, but before I outline them, it is important to reflect on Lohmeyer's aims as they had emerged so far. His projected seven-volume work on Early Christianity was planned to accompany his commentaries on the Gospels. A commentary on a Gospel can only deal with the text in the Gospels, and although there might be

---

[132] *Das Urchristentum*, p.38.

room for an Excursus or two, it would overbalance a commentary if an Excursus extended to 189 pages! The book on John the Baptist gave the rationale and ground for the treatment of the passages about John in the commentaries on Mark and Matthew.

If the resulting picture was fuller and more traditional than in New Testament scholarship, this was not because Lohmeyer was 'conservative'. It resulted from his pursuit of a critical-historical method, rather than an historical-critical method. It began from the phenomenon (in the case of John the Baptist the traditions in the Gospels, Acts, Josephus and the Church Fathers) and sought to account for the phenomenon. It did not try to reconstruct John's words and person on the basis of deciding which traditions were 'authentic' and which were not. There had to be an explanation even for the existence of material deemed to be not authentic. From this point of view, it is greatly to be regretted that Lohmeyer was not able to write the second volume in the proposed series, that on Jesus.

The second part of the book is entitled 'Preaching' and contains the following sections: John's arrival, God's wrath and Abraham's children, repentance, baptism, Spirit and fire baptism, the one baptising with water, works and rules, political impact, John's disciples, and John's death. It might be thought that this would involve repetition from the first part of the book, but this was not so. From the outset, questions were posed that needed an answer. For example, given that in contemporary Judaism it was believed that the era of prophecy had ended, how and why did the prophetic figure of John make such an obvious impact? Lohmeyer found a partial answer in the connection made in both Mark 1.2 and John 1.23 between the Baptist's mission and Isaiah 40.3: 'In the wilderness prepare the way of the Lord'. The wilderness had an eschatological significance in Judaism as the place where God sustained his people after the Exodus. Many Messianic pretenders had called the people to go to the wilderness, a place of holiness and purity. Lohmeyer could not know, of course, that the so-called 'Community Rule', discovered near the Dead Sea in 1947 shortly after his murder, included a reference to Isaiah 40.3 which further supported his case.[133]

The discussion of the meaning of John's baptism takes some unusual directions. Lohmeyer sought to ascertain what kind of involvement John had in the baptising process. Did the person being baptised immerse himself, or did John take part in the ceremony? If he did not take part, in what sense can we speak of John's baptism? Lohmeyer compared being baptised with bringing a sacrifice to the temple. In the latter case, a priest had necessarily to slaughter the animal, but the initiative came from the offerer, and the offering of the sacrifice was a matter between God and the offerer alone. Lohmeyer noted that, according to Mark 1.4, John 'preached a baptism of repentance', and concluded that whatever John might or might not have done in the ceremony, God was the true baptiser, not John.[134] In the later commentary on Mark, Lohmeyer would argue that despite Mark 1.5 saying that they were baptised by John, he took no part in the 'outward act'.[135] The baptism of each individual was a work of God, in which God bestowed, along with the washing, the gift of repentance. This line of reasoning enabled Lohmeyer to locate the word

---

[133] E. Lohse, *Die Texte aus Qumran*, Munich: Kösel Verlag, 1964 for the Hebrew text of 1 QS VIII, 14; English translation in G. Vermes, *The Complete Dead Sea Scrolls in English*, London: Allen Lane, 1992, p.109.

[134] *Das Urchristentum*, p.74, 'So ist auch nicht Johannes im letzten Sinne der Taufende, sondern Gott der wahre Täufer'.

[135] E. Lohmeyer, *Das Evangelium des Markus*, Göttingen: Vandenhoech & Ruprecht, 1937, p.16, 'Freilich, der Text spricht nicht von dem Tun der Täuflinge, sondern des Täufers ... trotzdem er an dem äußeren Akt der Taufe nicht beteiligt hat'.

and rite of baptism within the sphere of Judaism, albeit with a new meaning added by John.

If this was the nature of the water baptism, how did it relate to baptism with the Holy Spirit and fire that would be carried out by the 'one who was to come' (Matthew 3.11)? The 'one who was to come', and his baptism, belonged to the eschatological end. The person could thus not be named more precisely. Lohmeyer noted that recent exegesis had eliminated the reference to the Holy Spirit as 'inauthentic', but he saw no reason to do so.[136] The reference to the baptism of fire was to the eschatological judgement that would destroy all that was wicked and unholy. The baptism with the Holy Spirit referred to something that lay beyond the present world, to the realm of God, where everything was spirit. Lohmeyer quoted John 4.24: 'God is spirit'. All this raised in turn the question of the nature and person of John, which gave authority to the baptism as God's act and the words connected with it.

In the section on the person of the Baptist, Lohmeyer sought to elucidate the paradox of John being described as a prophet and as more than a prophet (Matthew 11.9). Was John a prophet? There is no account of him receiving a prophetic call as with some Old Testament prophets. Rather, the legend of the angelic announcement of his birth (Luke 1.11-20) lies much closer to non-prophetic Old Testament figures such as Isaac (Genesis 18.10). Again, Old Testament prophets say, typically, 'Thus saith the Lord'; John did not. Indeed, his 'I tell you' crossed the boundary between human and divine speech that 'thus saith the Lord' establishes. That John's identity was clearly a puzzle to the religious leaders of the time is reflected in the interrogation of John recorded in John 1.19-28, where he declared that he was not the Christ, nor Elijah, nor the prophet

---

[136] *Das Urchristentum*, p.84.

('like unto Moses'). Lohmeyer, as so often, resolved the paradox of John being a prophet and more than a prophet, by invoking the eschatological situation of which he was part. Because the new is coming he does not conform to the old or present situation. The baptism that he preaches is also something new. It takes its authority from John, but he gets his authority from it as something God-given, and whose efficacy depends precisely on the fact that the sacrificial system for cleansing from offerings, which it in a way supersedes, is also God given. John's use of the term 'now' (Matthew 3.10: 'Even now the axe is laid to the root of the trees') is also to be understood eschatologically. The 'now' is not yet, but the sign of what will be, just as water baptism is the necessary prelude to the coming of fire and spirit, factors that belong to the end.

John is thus an enigmatic figure. His sojourn in the wilderness and his asceticism are not paralleled in the Old Testament. Lohmeyer rejects any comparison with Elijah's sojourn at Mount Horeb or Zarephat (I Kings 17.9). His preaching is not like that of the Old Testament prophets, and the contemporary religious rulers are at a loss to understand him. The following words sum up Lohmeyer's account of John:

> [His message and work] place him in the solitariness of the wilderness in God's presence, so that before God he becomes tremblingly aware of his historical dependency, and precisely for this reason stands before his people with the authority that comes from beyond historical circumstances. For this reason he nowhere speaks of a divine mission, draws no distinction between his own words and those of God, and is more aware indeed of his own distance from God and the 'now' of a divine revelation than any prophet before him.[137]

---

[137] *Das Urchristentum*, p.102, 'Sie stellen ihn in die Wüsteneinsamkeit vor Gott, so dass er vor ihm aller geschichtlichen Gebundenheit sich zitternd bewußt wird und gerade deshalb vor seinem Volke in einer Autorität dasteht, die aus einem Jenseits des geschichtlichen Lebens herrüht. Darum spricht er an keiner

The remainder of this part of the book can be described in terms of a series of questions, to which the answer is 'no' and 'yes', and 'yes' and 'no'. This was the result of Lohmeyer's relentless logical perusal of different aspects of the traditions, and his refusal to try to reconstruct the person and work of John on the basis of subjective decisions about 'authentic' and 'inauthentic' historical traditions.

Did John expect his preaching and baptising to result in his being followed by disciples? At one level the answer was 'no'. He assumed that the soldiers and tax collectors who came to him for advice would resume their professions, and that the multitudes who came to him would resume their previous lives, following his advice to be compassionate to the poor (Luke 3.10-14).[138] In spite of this, his work attracted followers, whom he taught to pray (Luke 11.1) and who fasted (Mark 2.18), but did not otherwise appear to follow his ascetic way of life with its apparent wilderness roots. Also, Jesus and several of the first disciples seem to have been followers of John.

John's practical advice to the 'multitude', to the soldiers and to the tax collectors does not seem to have resembled the preaching of one who was baptising because he believed in the imminence of the 'end'. This was also true of his seemingly political involvement in the affairs of Herod Antipas, which led to his imprisonment and death. The preaching that was appropriate to someone anticipating an imminent end was 'repent and bear fruit that fits repentance'. But bearing fruit, although a type of human behaviour that at the end would be rewarded or punished, was also a divine work, as the notion of fruit implies: that it is something produced as a matter of

---

Stelle von einem göttlichen Auftrag, scheidet er nicht zwischen Gottes und seinen Worten und ist sich doch seiner eigenen Ferne von Gott und das "Jetzt" einer göttlichen Offenbarung tiefer bewußt als irgend ein Prophet vor ihm'.
[138] *Das Urchristentum*, pp.107-8.

course by the right kind of person. The fruit which results from repentance was possible only because God's revelation of repentance, effected through baptism, made it achievable.

Lohmeyer partly justified his complex, even at times contradictory, picture of John by allowing that the Synoptic Gospels concentrated on the public side of his work, while the Fourth Gospel spoke of things from the point of view of his followers, whose traditions were the source from which the Fourth Gospel was drawn.

In discussing the death of John the Baptist, Lohmeyer returned to the theme of martyrdom, so important in his commentaries on Philippians and Colossians. Lohmeyer based his argument partly on the saying of Jesus (Mark 9.13), 'I tell you that Elijah has come, and they did to him whatever they pleased, as it is written of him'. Significantly, the immediately preceding words referred to the Son of Man, and that he should suffer many things. According to Lohmeyer, this saying expressed the view either of Jesus or the Early Church that the death of John was a divinely-intended martyrdom that prefigured the death of Jesus. However, the question still needed to be raised as to whether martyrdom was implicit in John's mission. Here again, Lohmeyer turned to sayings of Jesus that linked baptism with martyrdom: 'Are you able to be baptised with a baptism with which I am baptised?' (Mark 10.38), and 'I came to cast fire on the earth ... I have a baptism to be baptised with' (Luke 12.49-50). These verses indicated a link between the ideas of water baptism, martyrdom and fire baptism and Lohmeyer felt that such ideas could not have been far from John's thoughts – that his baptising could lead to martyrdom and with it a baptism of fire.

The third part is entitled 'Presuppositions' and aims to elucidate the intellectual assumptions that underlay the mission of John, as understood by Lohmeyer. Particular attention was paid to the temple and priests, and the figure of Abraham as interpreted by Judaism. The occasion for this approach was two-fold. First, the traditions surrounding John's birth gave him a priestly genealogy (Luke 1.5-25 and 57-66). Second, his preaching warned that descent from Abraham was no automatic exemption from the coming judgement. The temple and its priesthood were God-given means of cleansing from offences. Also, the fate of the temple in Israel's history had eschatological significance; the same was true of the Jewish understanding of Abraham. Lohmeyer's aim was to demonstrate the Jewish roots of John's mission and message, although his mission and message inevitably moved beyond these roots. This was particularly clear in the case of the temple and its cult. The baptism of John made temple ministrations unnecessary. They had to be repeated, whereas John's baptism effected a once-and-for-all renewal. Lohmeyer juxtaposed the temple, the city and the land with what had come with John:

> There [that is, in the old order] the temple, the city and the land are holy; here [that is, with John], the wilderness beyond the boundaries. There, the traditional dress of the priests is holy; here, the dress that breaks with all traditions.[139] There, the various types of nourishment, prepared and enjoyed, are holy; here, it is the food and drink which no human hand has touched, but which the wildest nature has provided as though with good hands.[140]

---

[139] We have seen that Lohmeyer rejected the view that John's clothing evoked that of prophets such as Elijah. See p.130.

[140] Lohmeyer has in mind that John's food was locusts and wild honey (Mark 1.6). *Das Urchristentum*, p.126, 'Heilig ist dort der Tempel, die Stadt, das Land, hier die Wüste jenseits der Grenzen; heilig ist dort die überlieferte Tracht, hier das Gewand, das mit allen Traditionen bricht; heilig ist dort mannigfaltige Nahrung, in besondere Weise zubereitet und genossen; hier Speise und Trank,

Similarly, John's reference to Abraham was deeply rooted in the Jewish ideas, and yet was an attack on them:

> The Baptist's fight against the phrase, 'We have Abraham as our father', was also a fight against the divine institution of the cult and draws its compelling strength and meaning from this setting.[141]

Lohmeyer's discussion of repentance and baptism took a similar line. It sought to show how deeply rooted John's message was in the Jewish cultural thought-patterns and practices of his day, and yet how significantly different his words and works were. Baptism, for example, was deeply rooted in the need for ritual purification, and had a parallel in the baptism administered to proselytes, that is, to non-Jewish converts to Judaism. Yet John's baptism was different. Proselyte baptism brought a person into an historical community. John's baptism did not. Jewish baptismal and lustration rites also lacked the eschatological significance of John's baptism. This eschatological significance was also important for determining the form (*Gestalt*) of the Baptiser.

Lohmeyer distinguished between two forms of eschatological expectation in Judaism. One was centred upon the Messiah; but the Messiah was a human figure, a divine king, or a prophet like Moses or Elijah. The second form of hope was apocalyptic, such as that described in the book of Daniel, where a figure comes on the clouds of heaven (Daniel 7.13). For Lohmeyer, it was clear that John the Baptist set his hopes

---

die keines Menschen Hand berührt hat, sondern die ödeste Natur noch wie mit gütigen Händen unmittelbar spendet'.

[141] *Das Urchristentum*, p.135, 'So bedeutet des Täufers Kampf gegen den Satz, "Wir haben Abraham zum Vater", auch einen Kampf gegen die göttliche Institution des Kultes; und erst in dieser Zielrichtung gewinnt er seine aufwühlende Kraft und Bedeutung'.

on the second, the apocalyptic form, of the hope.[142] The consummation to which he looked was a priestly action, in that it had to do with baptism in spirit and fire. Lohmeyer quoted the Testament of Levi 18.1-4 as an example of the priestly apocalyptic figure behind John's expectations:

> And the Lord will raise up a new priest ...
> And his star shall rise in heaven like a king;
> Kindling the light of knowledge as day is illuminated by the sun ...
> He shall take away all darkness from under heaven
> And there will be peace in all the earth.[143]

Lohmeyer further linked the idea of the garments that would be worn by such a priest to the description of the Son of Man in Revelation 1.13: 'I saw one like the Son of Man, clothed with a long robe and with a golden girdle about his breast'.

The question of whether or not John the Baptist used the title 'Son of Man' is irrelevant to the fact that his thought was rooted in traditions and hopes centred on the Son of Man. Also part of the same complex of ideas was that of the Lamb of God. A reference to the Testament of Joseph 19.8 backed this up, being a description of a spotless lamb at whom all sorts of wild animals and reptiles rushed, but who were overcome and destroyed by the lamb.[144] This conclusion had a bearing on John 1.29, in which the Baptist says of Jesus, 'Behold, the Lamb of God'. For Lohmeyer, it was likely that John's Gospel was, at this point, recording an authentic utterance of the Baptist.[145] John's work and form could be

---

[142] *Das Urchristentum*, p.158, 'Für Johannes den Täufer ist es klar, dass er sich eindeutig der zweiten apokalyptischen Richtung angeschlossen hat'.

[143] H.C. Kee, 'The Testaments of the Twelve Patriarchs' in J. H. Charlesworth (ed.), *The Old Testament Pseudepigrapha. Vol. 1, Apocalyptic Literature and Testaments*, New York: Doubleday, 1983, p.794.

[144] 'Testament of Joseph' in Charlesworth, *Pseudepigrapha*, p.824.

[145] *Das Urchristentum*, p.160, note 2.

summarised as follows. It was an eschatologising of a priestly complex of ideas within Judaism. John was a high priest of baptism, which in turn was an eschatological priestly work of God.

What, then, of the tradition in the Synoptic Gospels that linked John with the figure of Elijah? Lohmeyer argued that this idea played no part in the Baptist's consciousness. Although Elijah obviously played a part in Jewish eschatological expectations, there was no link between Elijah and baptising. Further, according to John 1.21, the Baptist denied that he was Elijah returning. The link between John and Elijah owed its currency in the Synoptics to the saying of Jesus, 'If you are willing to accept it, he is Elijah who is to come' (Matthew 1.14). It did not reflect the Baptist's own understanding of his missionary work.

A final section entitled 'Significance' summed up all that had gone before in this remarkable book.

CHAPTER TWELVE

Galilee and Jerusalem

The preface to the book on John the Baptist was written in Breslau and dated October 1932. Lohmeyer's next major work, *Galilee and Jerusalem*, had a preface written in Greifswald and was dated Whitsun 1936.[146] He was no longer a professor in the prestigious University of Breslau, but now held his chair in the much smaller and less prestigious University of Greifswald. The events leading to his forcible removal to Greifswald are described by Köhn.[147] Because, among other things, Lohmeyer was a supporter of the Confessing Church, whose activities were increasingly declared to be illegal, he received an official order dated 15 October 1935, removing him from Breslau to Greifswald on account of his anti-National Socialist attitude and activity.

The beginning of his employment in Greifswald was to be April 1936, with leave to look for somewhere to live until 14 April. Whitsunday in 1936 fell on 31 May, so the preface to *Galilee and Jerusalem* was written very shortly after his move. One thing did not change. During his time in Breslau, the Lohmeyer family had had a country retreat in the tiny hamlet of Glasegrund, today Szklary, roughly 100 kilometres south of Wrocław. In fact, Lohmeyer was able to go there until well into 1944 before the Russian advance, and no doubt much of

---

[146] E. Lohmeyer, *Galiläa und Jerusalem* (Forschungen zur Religion und Literatur des Alten und Neuen Testaments, Neue Folge 34), Göttingen: Vandenhoeck & Ruprecht, 1936.
[147] Köhn, *Lohmeyer*, pp.87-93

his writing was also done there during the Greifswald years and whenever he had some respite during his military service from 1939 to 1943.

In some ways, *Galilee and Jerusalem* was ahead of its time, given the post-World War Two interest in the social background and setting of Early Christianity in Galilee and attention paid to the 'poor', the *'anavîm*.[148] Lohmeyer, however, did not set out in the first instance to address these matters, but to try to answer the question of why the New Testament located the Resurrection appearances of Jesus in Jerusalem (so Luke and John, ignoring chapter 21) and Galilee (so Matthew, and probably Mark). Because the New Testament saw Jerusalem as the place from which the earliest Church spread following the death and Resurrection of Jesus, it was widely held that the references to Galilee were not compatible with this, and were not to be regarded as historical evidence. Lohmeyer partly agreed with this but, typically, raised the question of why there were references to appearances in Galilee if they were not historical.[149] This led to a close examination of the accounts of the appearances of Jesus in the Gospels, in Paul's account in I Corinthians 15.3-8, and in some of the apocryphal gospels.

Lohmeyer's conclusions were that the prophecy in Mark 14.28, 'After I am raised up I will go before you to Galilee', and its enlargement in Mark 16.7, 'He has gone before you to Galilee', as well as Matthew 28.7, 'He is going before you to Galilee', followed by the great commission in Matthew 28.16-20, refer rather to the Parousia, the coming of Jesus in final judgment, than to an appearance of the Risen Lord to his followers.

---

[148] See S. Freyne, 'Galilee (Hellenistic/Roman)' in *Anchor Bible Dictionary*, vol. 2, pp.895-899.
[149] *Galiläa und Jerusalem*, pp.8-9, 14.

These passages referred to his lordship: 'All authority has been given to me' (Matthew 28.18). A similar point can be made about the references to Jesus's Jerusalem appearances. For example, the account in Luke 24.13-35 of the two disciples walking with the unrecognised Jesus to Emmaus was not so much about convincing the disciples that Jesus had overcome death, but about showing how his life and mission had been according to the Scriptures, which could now be seen in a new light. The appearance to the disciples in John 20.19-23 was similar to that at the close of Matthew, involving commissioning the disciples on the part of the One sent by the Father. This was also true of Luke 24.36-49, the meeting of Jesus with the disciples after the return of the Emmaus disciples to Jerusalem. Its purpose was to commission the disciples; they were to wait in Jerusalem until they were empowered from on high. The appendix to John's Gospel in chapter 21, with its Galilee appearance to seven of the disciples ended, again, with a commissioning, to Peter, to care for the Church. Lohmeyer was able to conclude that the accounts in the Gospels emphasised in different ways the accession of Jesus to power and authority, and the implication of this for the commission and mission of the Early Church. The *where* of the appearances (if that was how they should be described) was less important than their *significance*. This opened the way for the main purpose of the book, to consider the importance of Galilee for the mission of Jesus and the mission of the earliest Church.

The section entitled 'Galilee and Jerusalem in the story of Jesus'[150] examined each gospel in turn in relation to the part played by the locations of Galilee and Jerusalem in the accounts of the ministry of Jesus. A preliminary section pointed out that not only had Galilee been a centre for political

---

[150] *Galiläa und Jerusalem*, pp.25-46.

agitation against the Romans in the first century AD, but that following the fall of Jerusalem in AD 70, the centre of Judaism had shifted from Jerusalem to Galilee. At the time of the composition of the Gospels, Galilee was the new centre of the Jewish people and faith. Mark's Gospel, as was well known, divided neatly into two halves, the first (1.1 to 9.50) was located in Galilee including Sidon, the Decapolis and the region of Caesarea Philippi. The second part (10.1 to 16.8) was located in Judaea, beyond the Jordan and, finally, Jerusalem. Lohmeyer believed that there were passages in Mark that hinted that Jesus was familiar with the Jerusalem area before his final journey to the capital. He cited Mark 14.8 (the incident of his anointing in the house of Simon the leper in Bethany), and 14.49, 'Day by day I was with you in the temple teaching'. While these may not seem to provide compelling evidence for the point, they enabled Lohmeyer to draw the following important conclusion for his argument: that Mark's twofold division of the location of Jesus's ministry had other than historical grounds.[151] Whatever the historical reality might have been, Mark wanted to make the point that Galilee was the holy land of the Gospel message, and the place of its eschatological fulfilment. This was the meaning of the prophecy in Mark 14.28, 'I will go before you to Galilee'. This had not to do with a Resurrection appearance, but with the final consummation of Jesus's mission.

The incident of the calling of the first disciples by the Sea of Galilee, in what Lohmeyer called 'the preamble' to the Gospel of Mark, was scarcely in the right place chronologically, and indicated the priority of believing thought over historical accuracy.[152] In Mark 3.7-8, where crowds are said to have gathered to follow Jesus in Galilee from Judaea, Jerusalem,

---

[151] *Galiläa und Jerusalem*, p.28
[152] *Galiläa und Jerusalem*, p.30

Idumaea and beyond the Jordan, Galilee became the central gathering-point of his work. It made Galilee the place where Jesus established a new unity of the Jewish people, and where the eschatological gospel message was present.

There also emerges in this gospel a link between the secret of the Son of Man and the selection of Galilee. Mark's geography is dependent upon a theory of the Evangelist. In contrast to Galilee as the chosen holy place of the eschatological gospel message, Jerusalem appears in Mark as the place of sin and death.[153] While Matthew closely follows Mark geo-graphically, once the Holy Family has migrated to Nazareth from Bethlehem via Egypt, a passage from Isaiah 9.1-2 is quoted in Matthew 4.13-16, on which Lohmeyer laid especial emphasis:

> The land of Zebulon and the land of Naphtali,
> Toward the sea, across the Jordan,
> Galilee of the gentiles –
> The people who sat in darkness
> Have seen a great light,
> And for those who sat in the region and shadow of death,
> Light has dawned.

The items 'Galilee', 'Gentiles', and 'light', were significant for Lohmeyer. Galilee, the place of the non-Jews, has become a place of light and hope, and this was God's doing – and all this came together in one figure:

> Only the Son of Man is the *anatole ex hupsous*, the transcendent judge and lord of the world and at the same time a man among other men; the holy one among the unholy, the sinless among the sinful, the light in the darkness. Through him the Galilee of the heathen has become the land of the eschatological fulfilment.[154]

---

[153] *Galiläa und Jerusalem*, p.33
[154] *Galiläa und Jerusalem*, p.37, 'Nur der Menschensohn ist *anatole ex hupsous*, ist der tranzendente Richter und Herr der Welt und zugleich ein Mensch unter

Matthew's confirmation of Mark's view is strengthened by his placing of the Sermon on the Mount in Galilee, while the opposition to Jesus in Jerusalem is expressed more sharply (Matthew 23). On the other hand, Matthew does speak of Jerusalem as the Holy City in his narrative of the Temptations, and perhaps lightens Mark's preponderance of Galilee in the great commission at the end of the gospel, even if he agrees with Mark in placing the consummation in Galilee.

In John's Gospel, as is well known, the geographical split between Galilee and Jerusalem is more evenly spaced. There are, however, plenty of signs of antagonism between the two centres: 'Can any good thing come out of Nazareth?' asks Nathaniel at John 1.46; and at John 7.41 doubt is cast upon the truth of Jesus's works on the grounds that he comes from Galilee. Nicodemus is similarly rebuked when he speaks up for Jesus: 'Are you from Galilee too? Search and you will see that no prophet arises from Galilee' (John 7.32). However, Lohmeyer finds as the central geographical point in John's Gospel the contrast between the hiddenness of Jesus's mission in Galilee and its openness in Jerusalem. The crucial passage is at the beginning of John 7, where the brothers of Jesus rebuke him for doing secretly in Galilee what he should be doing openly in Jerusalem (John 7.1-9). When Jesus does work openly in Jerusalem, it is the place where he is glorified. Jerusalem becomes the centre of the gospel message only because Golgotha stands at its centre.[155]

Luke's Gospel is quite different. As well as Galilee and Jerusalem, Samaria plays a geographical part (Luke 9.51 to

---

anderen Menschen, ist der Heilige unter den Unheiligen, der Sündlose unter den Sündern, das Licht in der Finsternis. Darum ist durch ihn das Galiläa der Heiden zum Lande der eschatologischen Erfüllung geworden.'

[155] *Galiläa und Jerusalem*, p.41, 'So tritt Jerusalem nur darum in die Mitte des Evangeliums, weil Golgotha in seiner Mitte steht'.

18.14) and the Transfiguration, which is set in Galilee, has a definite Jerusalem reference (Luke 9.31: 'Moses and Elijah spoke of his departing which he was going to accomplish in Jerusalem'). In comparison with Mark, there is no mention in Luke of journeying to Tyre and Sidon, the Decapolis, or Caesarea Philippi. Luke's placement of the Parable of the Pounds (Luke 19.11-27) shows that Luke thought of Jesus as the Lord who would rule over Jerusalem. Other indicators (Luke 2.38, 'All who were looking for the redemption of Jerusalem') point to Jerusalem as the holy place for Luke. It is not surprising that the Easter stories are located there.

The fourth part of the book is entitled 'Galilee and Jerusalem in the Early Church' and seeks to establish two types of Early Christian belief and practice, one based in Jerusalem, the other in Galilee.[156] The principal source for the former is Luke and Acts. For Galilee, Lohmeyer is especially dependent on the work of Hegesippus, a Jewish Christian from Palestine or Samaria who lived in the second part of the second century AD, fragments of whose writings are quoted by Eusebius in his *Ecclesiastical History*, written early in the fourth century AD (around 303-317).

Lohmeyer pointed out that in the account of the beginnings of Christianity in Acts, Galilee was mentioned only once, in a summary phrase at 9.31: the gospel message is to be preached in Jerusalem, Judaea and Samaria but not, evidently, in Galilee. (Unless I have overlooked it, Lohmeyer makes no comment on the address to the disciples after Christ's Ascension by two men in white robes, 'Ye men of Galilee', Acts 1.11). A possible explanation for this apparent neglect of Galilee was the possibility that Luke thought that Galilee was

---

[156] *Galiläa und Jerusalem*, pp.47-79

already a Christian land, and could be deliberately omitted.[157] If this was the case, how had Galilee become a Christian land?

Lohmeyer believed that the family, that is, the brothers of Jesus and their offspring, were responsible for this missionary work. Paul had mentioned the brothers of the Lord, along with the other apostles and Cephas (Peter) at I Corinthians 9.5, implying that they were involved in the Christian mission. Hegesippus related how, under the persecutions of the Roman Emperor Domitian (AD 81-96) the grandson of Judah the brother of Jesus had been interrogated and had answered that Christ's kingdom was not of this world but that he would come in glory to judge the living and dead.[158] The missionary activity of the brothers of Jesus might also have been responsible for the spread of the gospel message to Damascus. Lohmeyer noted that Ananias, who laid hands upon Saul to recover his sight, is described in the accounts of Paul's conversion in Acts 22.12-16 as 'a devout man according to the law, well-spoken of by the Jews', and that he had said to Paul, 'The God of our fathers appointed you'. This indicated to Lohmeyer that Ananias was a Jewish Christian, who owed his Christian belief to Galilean missionaries related to Jesus. This suggestion led to an investigation of James the brother of Jesus and to the Nazarenes and the Ebionites.

A fragment in Hegesippus, quoted by Eusebius,[159] described James the brother of the Lord as one who, from birth, had drunk no wine, eaten no meat, and had not cut his hair. He went regularly to the temple to pray for forgiveness for his people, and was known as 'the Just'. Questioned by scribes and Pharisees about Jesus, he replied, 'Why do you ask me

---

[157] *Galiläa und Jerusalem*, p.52
[158] Eusebius, *Ecclesiastical History*, Book III, 17.20.
[159] Eusebius, *Ecclesiastical History*, Book II, 23.4-19. See also J. Stevenson, *A New Eusebius*, London: SPCK, 1957, pp.8-10.

about the Son of Man?' This seems to be a description of a Nazarite, that is, one who had taken a vow to separate or consecrate himself (Numbers 6.1-6). This vow could be permanent or temporary. At Acts 24.5 believers in Jesus are described as Nazarenes. This opens up a very complicated issue that cannot be pursued here. The basic question is whether Christians were so called because they followed Jesus of Nazareth, or is there some connection with a Jewish-Christian sect mentioned by the Church Fathers called Nazarenes?[160] Lohmeyer was aware of the difficulties, which he discussed fully, but felt that it was at least possible to conclude from the evidence that James represented a Galilean form of Christianity that understood Jesus in terms of the apocalyptic Son of Man. A further point had to do with poverty.

In several gospel incidents, Jesus enjoins poverty on those who would follow him. At Mark 10.17-31 Jesus tells the rich young ruler to sell all that he has. Peter says, 'We have left everything and followed you' (Mark 10.28). In Acts 4.32 to 5.11 the Christian community practises common ownership of goods and property. It seems that poverty was not a life-style choice for the earliest Christians, but a necessity. Lohmeyer goes back to the 'anavîm, the poor in the Psalms, and sees Jesus identifying himself with the poor; and he notes that there is a later connection through the earliest Christians to the Nazarenes and Ebionites ('evyon in Hebrew means 'poor') and into the Early Christian centuries. An interesting observation is that the Letter of James enjoins poverty (James 2.1-7). Its traditional ascription to James may reflect a link between James the brother of Jesus, and the practice of poverty.

---

[160] See the discussion in C.K. Barrett, *The Acts of the Apostles*, (International Critical Commentary), Edinburgh: T & T Clark, 1998, vol. 2, pp.1097-8.

The arguments of this section are too complex and detailed to be outlined here. They are summed up in the following words:

> In these pieces of ancient tradition the same Christology dominates that we found in James, arguably among the Nazarenes and also the grandchildren of the family of Jesus, even if somewhat less emphatic. Jesus is the eschatological teacher who, on the basis of the holy Jewish law and particular commandments (poverty and discipleship) and divine power leads his own people through the door of the kingdom of God. He is now exalted to God's right hand and will soon return with the 'clouds of heaven' as judge of the world.[161]

That the fragments in Hegesippus in which James mentions the Son of Man have preserved an ancient tradition is indicated, according to Lohmeyer, by the fact that in the New Testament, the Son of Man concept in its Daniel 7 form is mentioned only in Mark 13.26 and parallels, and in Revelation 1.13 and 14.14. In contrast to the Galilean type of primitive Christian belief, that of Jerusalem was richer in its portrayal of Jesus as the Messiah and the outpouring of the Holy Spirit. This was the view of the Acts of the Apostles and of its spokesman Peter. The two types of Resurrection appearance narratives reflected Galilean (Mark/Matthew) and Jerusalem perspectives (Luke, with John combining them).

In a final section,[162] Lohmeyer attempted a sketch of the development of Early Christianity. It began in Galilee with Jesus and came from the circles of the poor, teaching loyalty to

---

[161] *Galiläa und Jerusalem*, p.74, 'So herrscht auch in diesen Stücken alter Überlieferung die gleiche Christologie, die wir bei Jakobus fanden, bei den Nazoräern vermuteten und bei der Enkeln der Familie Jesu noch, wenn auch dünner geworden, bezeugt sehen. Jesus ist der eschatologischer Lehrer, den von dem Grunde des heiligen jüdischen Gesetzes aus durch besondere Gebote (Armut und Nachfolge) und göttlichen Macht die Seinen zur Tür des Gottesreiches führt; er ist jetzt zur Rechten Gottes erhöht und wird in Bälde kommen als Weltenrtichter "mit den Wolken des Himmels".'
[162] *Galiläa und Jerusalem*, pp.80-104.

the Jewish law plus the need for poverty and discipleship. Lohmeyer noted that there were differences in how the law was interpreted and practised between Galilee and other parts of the country. His mission was to Galilee, and the cursing of Capernaum (Matthew 11.23) was an indication that this part of the land was made holy by his mission and would therefore suffer more greatly in the Day of Judgement.

It was possible to reconstruct from the Gospel of Mark what Lohmeyer called 'the piety' of the Galilean Early Christian community. The following incidents were basic:

I   The raising of Jaïrus's daughter (5.21-24, 35-43)
II   The Feeding of the 5,000 (6.34-44)
III The Syro-Phoenician woman (7.24-30)
IV   The Transfiguration (9.2-8)

The 'sayings source' contained the following traces: the rich young ruler and the sayings about leaving all to follow Jesus (Mark 10.17-27) and possibly the sayings about entering the narrow gate (Matthew 7.13-14); in the Passion narrative, the Entry into Jerusalem, the Cleansing of the Temple, the celebration of the Passover,[163] the story of Gethsemane, the Sanhedrin trial, parts of the Crucifixion narrative, and the rending of the veil of the temple. This Galilean tradition was the basis for the mission of the family of Jesus, and of James his brother, who became the effective head of the community in Jerusalem. He took the lead at the Council of Jerusalem (Acts 15.13-21) and sent representatives to Antioch to see that Peter was kept in order (Galatians 2.11-12). He was putting into effect the loyalty to the law that was a feature of the Galilean understanding of Early Christianity.

---

[163] Lohmeyer noted the polemic of Origen against the Nazarenes, who defended the Last Supper as a Passover meal. *Galiläa und Jerusalem*, p.88.

Lohmeyer saw Luke as responsible for championing the Jerusalem understanding of the mission of Jesus, possibly deriving it from the circle of Jesus's disciples, as opposed to his family. Its constellation of the holiness of Jerusalem, Jesus as Messiah, and the outpouring of the Holy Spirit were its distinguishing features which did not, however, completely obscure the Galilean element, particularly as represented by James the brother of Jesus. A possible new development of the Galilean understanding lies in the figure of Stephen. He displays some of the features of Galilean Christianity: the rejection of the temple and the vision of the Son of Man at the right hand of God (Acts 7.2-56). On the other hand he had a more negative view of the Jewish law. Another strand in the development of Early Christian belief comes from the movement stemming from John the Baptist and his followers. Lohmeyer saw a unifying factor in these various emphases, in the proclamation by Jesus of the imminence of the Kingdom of God and the future hopes to which this proclamation gave rise. The Early Christian community did not have a single unified origin or line of development. In various ways it developed out of the two centres that feature in the Gospels and Acts: Galilee and Jerusalem.

CHAPTER THIRTEEN

The Commentaries on Mark and Matthew and the Book on the Lord's Prayer

It will seem strange that while previously in this book whole chapters have been devoted to texts of less than a hundred, or less than two hundred pages, the present chapter will deal with three works totalling some one thousand pages! The reason is that, as previously pointed out, Lohmeyer's commentaries are so packed with information and detailed interpretation of the biblical text that there is no way in which they can be adequately described or summarised. They have to be read, which for most of the intended readers of this book will not be possible because of the language barrier. The book on the Lord's Prayer does exist in English translation, and will be described later in the chapter. All that will be possible with regard to the commentaries will be to select some passages and to outline how Lohmeyer dealt with them.

In partial mitigation it can be said that previous chapters have covered some of the general background to the commentaries. Lohmeyer's introduction to *John the Baptist* dealt with his approach to the critical-historical treatment of Gospel narratives. *Galilee and Jerusalem* contained an introduction to Mark's Gospel, as well as an account of how Lohmeyer understood the mission of Jesus and the development of Early Christianity. And, returning to the book on John the Baptist, there was there a thorough treatment of Lohmeyer's reconstruction of the Baptist's ministry, including the importance of the traditions in John's Gospel. Lohmeyer's basic convictions, set out in the earlier works and written while he was working on the commentary on Mark, did not change, although in the commentaries his close engagement with the text often produced surprising, and typically individualistic, interpretations and comments.

A word needs to be said about the commentary on Matthew. To say that it was unfinished when Lohmeyer was murdered is to understate the situation. According to Lohmeyer's pupil Werner Schmauch, who edited the commentary, only chapters 21 and 22 existed in a form suitable for publication, while material for chapters 6, 7, 10, 11 and 24 was wholly lacking. Other fragments written during and after military service existed as unconnected pieces in odd notebooks or on army postal materials. In the event, Schmauch succeeded in putting together something that resembles a proper commentary, albeit one with gaps at certain points, amounting to 430 pages. While it is obviously not the work that Lohmeyer would have overseen had his life not been brutally cut short, it is an astonishingly authentic representation of Lohmeyer's thought and achievement, a costly treasure rescued from near oblivion.

Because Lohmeyer's expositions could sometimes go radically against the consensus of preceding scholarship, it will be useful to begin with a case where this was not so, the commentary on Mark 2.1-11. In his commentary on Mark published in 1925, A.E.J. Rawlinson had followed earlier scholars in dividing the passage into two sections: 2.1-5a, 12, in which Jesus heals a lame man; and 2.5b-10, an altercation between Jesus and 'certain of the scribes', provoked by Jesus's claim to be able to forgive sins.[164] Lohmeyer agreed with this, pointing out that the conclusion, in which the witnesses to the

---

[164] A.E.J. Rawlinson, *The Gospel according to St Mark*, (Westminster Commentaries), London: Methuen, 1925, pp.23-27

miracle were astonished and glorified God, made no mention of the immediately-preceding controversy. Lohmeyer also remarked that nowhere else was the forgiveness of sins attributed to the Son of Man, and that the passage 2.5b-10 must have originated from the claim of the Early Christian community that Jesus, whom it saw as the Son of Man, had power to forgive sins granted to him by God; this was in opposition to Jewish beliefs that only a priest, by means of sacrifice, had the power to pronounce forgiveness, not to an individual, but to the people as a whole.

This by no means exhausts what Lohmeyer makes of the passage! One of the features of his Gospel commentaries is what today would be called a narrative approach or literary reading, without these things being consciously invoked. We are invited, as it were, to join the people in the house where Jesus is teaching and where the lame man is brought by his friends. We are invited to join those present in their reaction to the work of healing, to see Jesus as a fulfilment of the promise of Isaiah 61.1, as the One to whom God has given power and authority to work the divine will.

The interpolated scene raises other questions. What is the relation between illness and sin, and are the sufferer or his fathers responsible for it? What does it mean to forgive sins, and is it easier or harder to do this than to effect healing? The juxtaposition of the two episodes means that they affect each other. Jesus, as the one with authority to forgive sins, becomes more than a prophet, fulfilling Isaiah 61.1. The divine power and authorisation implicit in the healing anchors Jesus as the One who can forgive sins in an Old Testament understanding of God, which preserves its monotheism while affirming the divine nature of the mission of Jesus. Characteristically,

Lohmeyer looks for theological motives underlying the mechanics of the formation of the Gospel tradition.

Lohmeyer's treatment of the Transfiguration (Mark 9.2-8) could only have been written by him. The account originated, whether as a visionary portrayal, genuine memory or believing legend, in the 'poor' circles of Galilean Christianity.[165] Lohmeyer was particularly struck by the observation that the whiteness of the garments was such as no fuller could produce (Mark 9.3), which pointed, for him, to village life in Galilee. However, whatever the origins of the passage, it contained profound theological significance. Its placement on a mountain linked it to Old Testament 'appearances' of God on Mount Sinai and Mount Horeb, and the time-reference of six days (Mark 9.2) indicated the time of preparation needed for the divine revelation (Exodus 24.16). Also, the location of the mountain in Galilee confirmed Galilee as the land of the Gospel for the writer of Mark, and also undermined the claim of Mount Zion (i.e., Jerusalem) to be the centre of God's revelation. The three disciples who witnessed the Transfiguration, Peter, James and John, were important in several respects. First, Peter, their spokesman, was the character through whom the narrator of the passage could pose questions and indicate reactions. Second, it was significant that only they, and not the Twelve or a larger number of disciples, were present. This meant that a clear revelation of the true nature of the Son of Man nevertheless remained hidden, except to a few. In a typical paradoxical observation, Lohmeyer remarked that Jesus, manifestly a human being and a hidden Lord, becomes in this moment a manifest Lord and a hidden human being.[166]

---

[165] E. Lohmeyer, *Das Evangelium des Markus* (Kritisch-exegetischer Kommentar über das Neue Testament), Göttingen: Vandenhoeck & Ruprecht, 1937, p.178.
[166] Lohmeyer, *Mark*, p.179, 'Er ist offenbar Mensch und verborgener Herr und wird in diesem Augenblick offenbarer Herr und verborgener Mensch'.

Several features contribute to the 'revelation': the cloud (and compare Exodus 19.16), the whiteness (compare the face of Moses which glowed after his meeting with God on Mount Sinai, Exodus 34.29), and the presence of Moses and Elijah who were present, not as prefiguring the 'end', but as part of the end that was beginning. The voice from heaven, 'This is my beloved Son, hear him' (Mark 9.7), was also crucial and defined the Transfiguration in relation to the Baptism of Jesus, and to the Resurrection.

The link with the Baptism was obvious because of the voice from heaven that said, 'Thou art my beloved Son in whom I am well pleased' (Mark 1.11). But the Transfiguration went beyond the Baptism in that it gave content to the message of the heavenly voice, and revealed the hiddenness of Christ's lordship in his manhood. In relation to the Resurrection, Lohmeyer noted that no Resurrection narrative emphasised the lordship of Jesus in the way that the Transfiguration did. Lohmeyer also noted that in Mark and Matthew (otherwise in Luke 9.31) the Transfiguration was not linked to the death of Jesus. What was emphasised was Jesus's teaching, with the divine word, 'Hear him!' The end result was that the Transfiguration narrative was a kind of independent tradition, stemming from Galilean 'poor' Christian circles, expressing profound theological insights against an Old Testament background, and placed at the pivotal point in Mark's portrayal of Jesus as the Son of Man.

Lohmeyer's treatment of the Passion narrative of Mark 14-15 brought together his skills as an historian, a literary critic and a theologian, and it is an object lesson in how he combined them. Any commentator on this narrative has to face difficult historical questions. Who, if anyone, made or kept a record of the trial of Jesus, and if no one did, where did the gospel narrative come from? Is it credible that a high Roman official such as Pontius Pilate would personally deal with the trial of an unimportant Jew? What is to be made of the chronological difficulties of the narrative, including the apparent conflict between Mark and John's Gospels about whether or not the Last Supper was a Passover meal? Lohmeyer was well aware of these and other difficulties, as well as the fact that some scholars, principally but not solely Bultmann, regarded much of the material in the Passion narrative as unhistorical, and had described, for example, the account of the institution of the Last Supper as a cult legend of the Hellenistic circles around Paul.[167]

Lohmeyer was more cautious. In *Galilee and Jerusalem* he had argued that Mark's division of his Gospel into two sections, the first in Galilee, the second in Jerusalem, was dictated by theology and not history, and he had drawn attention to hints in Mark that Jesus's visit to Jerusalem for his Passion was not his first time in the capital. It was likely that the 'Holy Week' narrative incorporated traditions about earlier incidents in Jerusalem, and the exact chronological relationship of some 'Holy Week' incidents to others could not be determined.[168] Also, it was necessary for the proclamation, 'Christ died for our sins', to become a narrative. This did not mean that it had no basis in factuality, although legendary elements in the narrative, such as the 'finding' of the animal for the Entry into Jerusalem and the mysterious preparations for the Last Supper, pointed, theologically, to the divinely-guided process whereby the Son of Man fulfilled his eschatological mission.

---

[167] R. Bultmann, *The History of the Synoptic Tradition*, trans. J. Marsh, Oxford: Blackwell, 1968, p.265.
[168] Lohmeyer, *Mark*, p.285.

The Last Supper, even if Mark supposed it to be a Passover meal, in fact bore no relationship to such a meal and invoked none of its features.[169] Its function was to sustain the eschatological community that Jesus had established in his lifetime, so that it extended beyond his death and incorporated the mission of the Son of Man. However, the belief that the death of Jesus was a necessary realisation of the sufferings of the Son of Man was not an invention of the post-Easter community, but came from Jesus himself.[170] The Last Supper was, in fact, the origin of the Christian Church.

Lohmeyer traced the story of Gethsemane to the Son of Man traditions of the Galilean 'poor' circles, the story of Peter's denial to Peter himself,[171] while information about Jesus's hearing before the Sanhedrin could owe details to sympathisers such as Joseph of Arimathea and Nicodemus.[172] Yet to draw attention to these facts is to do less than justice to Lohmeyer. His observations about the possible historical grounding of aspects of the Passion narrative, important though they were, came at the end of his theological expositions, and were printed in much smaller type. The expositions themselves were, as ever, full of surprises and unusual insights as Lohmeyer drew out the implications of the phrase, 'the Son of Man must suffer', the contrasts between the hiddenness of the mission and identity of the Son of Man, and the universal implications of what he was to bring about. Again, the frailty of his followers illustrated the other part of

---

[169] *Mark*, p.309.
[170] *Mark*, p.310, 'So gewiß aber dieser Tod Jesu nicht erst in der Verkündung der Urgemeinde, sondern nach Seinem eigenen Wort eines göttlichen "Muß" gehorcht, so gewiß ist auch die Jüngergemeinschaft in ihrer eschatologischen Bedeutung und Wirklichkeit nicht abgebrochen, sondern damit bis zu jenem Tage' [Lohmeyer is referring to Mark 14.25, 'I shall not drink again ... until *that day* when I drink it new in the Kingdom of God'] der Vollendung'.
[171] *Mark*, p.333, 'Um solchen theologischen Gründen willen besteht kein Hindernis, die Erzählung auf den Bericht des Petrus selbst zurückzuführen'.
[172] *Mark*, p.331

the phrase that the Son of Man would be 'given into the hands of sinful men'.

Lohmeyer's handling of the prayer of Jesus in the Garden of Gethsemane is a good example of his exegesis, and is also important in view of what will be said later in this chapter about Lohmeyer's book on the Lord's Prayer. For Lohmeyer, the death of Jesus was a martyrdom, albeit a unique one, because of the person of the martyr. In his treatment of Mark 10.38-9 he had written that 'martyrdom did not depend upon human volition or ability, but that it was a divinely given duty and privilege'.[173] Granted this, the prayer of Jesus in Gethsemane was not that of someone oppressed by fears of a future whose only outcome would involve suffering and possibly death. It was the prayer of one who looked forward to fulfilling what was the divinely given duty and privilege. The phrase 'cup' had, as in the Old Testament background, the idea of the 'cup of suffering'. Lohmeyer presumably had in mind a passage such as Isaiah 51.16-23; and, since 'cup' also implied 'feast', Lohmeyer wrote that in this 'hour', God's hour, Jesus was being invited to the guest meal of suffering.[174] The account could be compared to that of the Transfiguration, in which God made known his purpose and will to one who was more than a prophet. In turn, this affected how the phrase, 'Yet not what I will, but what thou wilt' (Mark 14.36), should be translated and understood. Lohmeyer proposed to render this as, 'It is not to question what I want, but what you want'.[175] The phrase was thus not an expression of submission, but a statement of what was a fact. It resembled the third petition of the Lord's Prayer, 'Thy will be done'.

---

[173] *Mark*, p.222, 'Ein Märtyrertum [hängt] nicht an menschlichen Willen oder Können, sondern gottgegebene Pflicht und Gnade ist'.
[174] *Mark*, p.315.
[175] *Mark*, p 316,'Es ist nicht zu fragen, was Ich will, sondern was Du'.

The other passage prayed by Jesus in the Passion narrative is the word from the Cross, 'My God, my God, why hast thou forsaken me?' (Mark 15.34). Lohmeyer wrote that no attempt should be made to lessen or minimise the sense of abandonment that these words express. At this moment, the world is empty of God. Yet this cry of abandonment, by using the words 'my God', becomes the closest possible affirmation of nearness to God. Further, the fact that the words come from Psalm 22 indicates that Jesus's sufferings on the Cross are the eschatological fulfilment of all the sufferings and doubts expressed in the Psalms and the prophetic books of the Old Testament. They give depth and content to the words 'the Son of Man must suffer'. At this moment of total doubt, he becomes the eschatological victor over death and over all powers that seek to resist God.[176]

As he wrote the commentary on Mark, Lohmeyer was evidently thinking about its follow-up, the commentary on Matthew. This is evident from his treatment of the Parable of the Sower in Mark 4.3-9 and Matthew 13.3-9, together with the interpretation of the parable in Mark 4.14-20 and Matthew 13.18-23, and with the intervening material about the reasons for Jesus's teaching in parables and the enigmatic reference to Isaiah 6.9-10. The commentary on Mark devoted three pages to these passages; that on Matthew extended to nearly fourteen!

About the time that Lohmeyer was thinking about the interpretation of this and other parables, the standard view in New Testament scholarship was that parables were not allegories, that is, that their meaning was to be sought primarily at the surface level of the story, and that the individual characters and incidents in parables did not have

---

[176] *Mark*, p.346

deeper meanings. C.H. Dodd's book, *The Parables of the Kingdom*, published in 1935 and therefore almost contemporary with Lohmeyer's commentary on Mark, had an introduction in which he criticised among other things the allegorical way in which the explanation of the Parable of the Sower in Mark 4.14-20 misunderstood and misrepresented the parable itself.[177] The mistake had been to identify each type of soil in the parable with a type of human response to the hearing of the message of the Gospel. Lohmeyer cared little for standard conventions of scholarship, and as usual went his own way in his interpretation of the parable.

Another unusual, but characteristic feature of his commentary, was the way in which he took seriously the interpretation of the parable in Mark 4.14-20, closely followed by Matthew 13.18-23, to which Lohmeyer devoted much space. It had long been accepted that if the parable itself was an authentic word of Jesus, the interpretation could not be so. Rawlinson wrote, 'It is difficult not to think that what is here presented to us is rather the way in which the parable was currently applied when Mark was written than any authentic word of Jesus'.[178] Lohmeyer was not worried by this, because his task was to interpret the tradition as it stood in the Gospels, the tradition being evidence for the phenomenon of Early Christianity.

In interpreting the parable itself, Lohmeyer was worried by features in it that seemed to suggest that it was far from being a simple account of a man sowing seed. It was often suggested that in ancient Palestine seed was sown before the soil was ploughed, and that this was why the seeds that fell on the path were devoured by birds. The path had not been ploughed before the seeds were eaten up. Yet the fact of later ploughing

---

[177] C.H. Dodd, *The Parables of the Kingdom*, London: Nisbet, 1935, pp.12-13
[178] Rawlinson, *Mark*, pp.52-3. Compare Dodd, *Parables*, p.13.

could not apply either to the stony or the weed-infested ground, and in any case there was no mention of ploughing in the parable. Again, was it true to the facts that the seed falling in stony soil would spring up *immediately* (Matthew 13.5, Greek *eutheôs*)? This led Lohmeyer to argue that the parable was not about simple agricultural sowing, but about a concrete eschatological event, and less about types of soil and more about the 'ground' of human hearts. In other words, Lohmeyer saw in the parable deeper implications, implications that would be further explored in the interpretation of verses 18-23.

Yet, in dealing with the interpretation, Lohmeyer concentrated not upon different types of human being, such as the superficial, the hard-hearted, the care-ridden and the good. He was concerned with the fate of the seed, and the different types of soil were necessary only as the indicators of the situation in which the eschatological message of the Kingdom was preached and heard. So far as human hearts (whole persons) were concerned, they were only what God had made them. There was nothing in the parable about human activity, or rewards. In the case of the words 'choked by thorns' (weeds) the association of this episode with cares (Matthew 13.22) indicated that the preached message came into a world that was governed by the principle of cares. It did not refer to the cares that oppress individuals in their daily lives:

> Care is an inverted relationship. It knows only itself and does not see that truth and life cohere only in what care is not. Similarly, the world is essentially self-absorbed and to that extent alienated from what it ought to be, namely, the work of its Creator, 'the Other', who stands over it and gives it life and substance.[179]

---

[179] Lohmeyer, *Matthew*, p.209, 'Sorge ist die Bezogenheit auf sich; sie kennt nur sich und sieht nicht, dass nur in dem, was sie nicht ist, Wahrheit und Leben ist. So ist also die Welt ihrem Wesen nach selbstbezogen und damit dem

This observation is typical of the points that Lohmeyer extracted from the text, whether they were intended or not, and show why reading the commentary is such an illuminating exercise.

In the difficult passage on why it was necessary for Jesus to speak in parables (Matthew 13.10-17), Lohmeyer made important claims that he had also elaborated in an article published in 1938, entitled 'On the meaning of the parables of Jesus'.[180] He claimed that the parables were themselves eschatological events, which contained the mystery of the hiddenness of the Kingdom of God in the present world. They thus had a double face, whose deeper, eschatological sense was available to those who were granted access to this secret or mystery (Matthew 13.10-12), but not to those 'outside'. This was why it was necessary for the Kingdom to be preached by means of parables; it also justified Lohmeyer's insistence on swimming against the tide of contemporary New Testament scholarship in seeking deeper meaning in the parables.

A quite different aspect of the Matthew commentary can be seen in Lohmeyer's treatment of the episode of the Syro-Phoenician woman (Matthew 15.21-38), which also occurs in Mark 7.24-30. The usual view is that Mark was the source for Matthew's account which, however, was extensively rewritten by Matthew.[181] Lohmeyer took a different view. Matthew's

---

entfremdet, was sie sein sollte, das Werk ihres Schöpfers, "des Anderen", der über ihr steht und ihr Leben und Bestand gibt'.

[180] E. Lohmeyer, 'Vom Sinn der Gleichnisse Jesu' in *Zeitschrift für systematische Theologie* 15 (1938) pp.319-346, reprinted in Lohmeyer, *Urchristliche Mystik. Neutestamentliche Studien*, Darmstadt: Wissenschaftliche Buchgesellschaft, 1958, pp.123-157.

[181] See, for example, J. Gnilka, *Das Matthäusevangelium. 2. Teil 14, 1-28, 20*, Darmstadt: Wissenschaftliche Buchgesellschaft, 2000, pp.28-29; U. Luz, *Das Evangelium nach Matthäus (Mt. 8-17)*, Zürich: Benzinger Verlag; Neukirchen-Vluyn: Neukirchener Verlag, 1990, pp.430-1. Luz speaks of Matthew's account as possessing 'high literary quality'.

account was independent, and Lohmeyer paid special attention to the differences between the two narratives. For example, whereas in Mark 7.25 the privacy of Jesus is invaded by a woman entering the house where Jesus is taking refuge, an unlikely thing for a non-Jewish woman to do, in Matthew the woman appears to accost Jesus in the street. Another difference is that, in Mark, Jesus seems to have granted the woman's wish for her daughter to be healed solely on the basis of her reply about the dogs eating crumbs that fall from the table. In Matthew, Jesus says explicitly, 'Great is your faith. Be it done to you as you desire'.

Lohmeyer also interprets the dialogue between Jesus and the woman differently in Matthew from his interpretation in the commentary on Mark. In Mark, Jesus says, 'Let the children first be fed' (Mark 7.27). For Lohmeyer, this meant that Jesus was to be seen as the father of the children spoken of, in contrast to the little dogs who represented non-Jews. Lohmeyer also detected a 'Johannine' sense in Jesus as the bread of life, as well as a Galilean Jewish tendency of belief (*Glaubensrichtung*) behind the words.

A notable difference between the two accounts is that, in Matthew, the woman's initial cry for help is met, first by silence on the part of Jesus, and secondly, with a request from the disciples that she should be sent away. Lohmeyer saw in the silence of Jesus an indication of the hiddenness of his mission; but it was also a hint and a movement on his part towards the mother. The disciples also got an answer to their request. The woman was sent away, but not in the manner the disciples wanted.

In Matthew, when Jesus gives his first answer to the woman, it is, 'I was sent only to the lost sheep of the house of Israel'

(Matthew 15.24). These words had many resonances: with the mission charge to the disciples ('Go to the lost sheep of the house of Israel', Matthew 10.6), with the passage in I Kings 22.17 ('I saw all Israel scattered...as sheep that have no shepherd'), and to the vision in Ezekiel 34 of God seeking his sheep. This meant that Jesus was seeing things through God's eyes. The words betrayed a Galilean Christology, rooted in the idea of the Son of Man and his task to seek and restore the lost. The woman's reply to Jesus in Matthew differed significantly from that in Mark in one small point. In Mark she says, 'Even the dogs under the table eat the children's crumbs' (7.28); in Matthew the words are, 'Even the dogs eat the crumbs which fall from their master's table' (15.27). In Matthew, there is no hint that the domestic dogs may be taking food away from the children. The crumbs are legitimately meant for the little dogs. Jesus is seen to be the Lord who presides at his table, before whom the woman stands, and whose faith in him is to be rewarded. A great privilege is bestowed upon her when Jesus addresses her as 'woman' (verse 28), an address elsewhere found only twice, in addresses of Jesus to his mother (John 2.4, 19.26). Lohmeyer's treatment of the passage well illustrates his practice that, whatever elements may make up the passage, it must be treated as a 'monad', a unique composition requiring a uniquely appropriate interpretation.

Whilst working on his commentary on Matthew during military service, Lohmeyer was also writing his book on the Lord's Prayer, which he was able to complete after his discharge from military service. The manuscript was delivered to Vandenhoeck & Ruprecht in Göttingen by hand by Lohmeyer's son Helmut, towards the end of October 1945.[182] By the time that it appeared in 1946, Lohmeyer was

---

[182] Köhn, *Lohmeyer*, p.123.

incommunicado, and the book was published without the usually expected foreword by the author.

Many of Lohmeyer's preoccupations can be found in the book. The fact that the prayer could be divided into seven parts in its version in Matthew, with the fourth part – that concerning 'bread for the morrow' being pivotal – echoed the Revelation commentary and the scheme in Stefan George's *The Seventh Ring*.[183] This pattern was significant even if Matthew had lengthened Luke's version or Luke had shortened Matthew's version. In fact, Lohmeyer argued that the two versions stemmed from two different streams of oral tradition of preaching, going back to Jesus, the one, Matthew, deriving from Galilee, the other, in Luke, from Jerusalem. It was a mistake to try to reconstruct an original form from the two versions, and Lohmeyer was sharply critical of Harnack's attempt to do this. There was no 'original form'.[184]

The expositions of the individual petitions were uniquely those of Lohmeyer, and need not be illustrated here, given that there is an English translation of the book. The point to which I want to draw attention comes at the end of the book, and concerns the nature and importance of prayer.

In Hönigswald's chapter on the problem of belief in his *Basic Questions of Epistemological Theory*, there are some interesting passages concerning prayer.[185] These follow several pages in which Hönigswald makes some trenchant criticisms of 'dialectical theology', without naming its advocates. Presumably he had Karl Barth in mind and the latter's

---

[183] E. Lohmeyer, *Das Vater-unser*, Göttingen: Vandenhoeck & Ruprecht, 1946, pp.194-5; ET *The Lord's Prayer*, London: Collins, 1965, pp.274-5.
[184] *Vater-unser*, p.207, English, p.291.
[185] R. Hönigswald, *Grundfragen der Erkenntnistheorie*, Tübingen: J.C.B. Mohr (Paul Siebeck), 1931, pp.151-2.

aversion to philosophy, his stress on the sinfulness of human nature and the limitations of human knowledge, so that God can only be known in his revelation. Hönigswald objects to what he calls an 'illegitimate use' of the notion of dialectic, whose traditional purpose is to gain knowledge by critically examining the ambiguities implied in notions. As used by dialectical theology, the purpose of the dialectics is to create an impassable barrier between God and humanity.[186] The 'sinfulness' of which it speaks cannot be a separation from God, but only something that exists in relation to God.[187] Dialectical theology cannot be 'scientific' because it operates with a defective and unexamined notion of 'givenness', that is, what is epistemologically involved in the apprehension of an object (*Gegenstand*). Belief in God has its roots not in a denial of humanity, but in the positive appreciation of the failures of humanity to fulfil the obligations that it experiences as duties and calls to realisation.

'God' is in the first instance a culturally-transmitted object who is experienced as a 'thou'. 'I experience God in his distance from me, and what I am in my distance from him'.[188] 'As a sinner I lift myself to him, and overcoming my sinfulness I affirm him, my sinfulness and my own self'.[189] Prayer comes into this because the 'I' speaks to God, and in this way the 'I' transcends its cultural and historical embeddedness, because God is the Unconditioned. This is what helps to make the 'I'

---

[186] Hönigswald, *Grundfragen*, p.149, 'Der dialektische Theologe in dem modernen Sinn dieses Wortes errichtet zwischen Gott und dem Menschen einen schlechthin unübersteigbaren Wall'.

[187] *Grundfragen*, p.149, 'Allein, "Sündhaftigkeit", was ist das ohne den Glaubensbezug Gottes und das Glaubenserlebnis des im Begriff der Kultur definierten "Menschen"'

[188] *Grundfragen*, p.151,' Ich erlebe Gott in seinem Abstande von mir, mich in meinem Abstande von ihm'.

[189] *Grundfragen*, p.151, 'Als "Sünder" erhebe ich mich zu ihm und in der Überwindung meiner "Sündhaftigkeit" bejahe ich ihn, meine Sündhaftigkeit und mich selbst'.

what it is. Prayer mirrors the theoretical content of faith. It is also a means by which the 'I' receives divine grace. In all this, we might say that Hönigswald is constructing a religion of reason, one which takes full account of the religious experiences of cultures and individuals, experiences which are not to be explained away, but to be accounted for rationally in the context of a philosophy that takes seriously all forms of human encounter with objects and the epistemological implications of these encounters.

Lohmeyer points out that Christianity is unique among religions, in that it has as its defining feature a particular prayer, the Lord's Prayer.[190] He acknowledges, of course, that other religions, especially Judaism, have a prayer or prayers; but the Lord's Prayer is special in that it discloses the drawing near of God's eschatological final purpose. To put the matter in ideas drawn from Hönigswald, we can say that because of its particular content, the Lord's Prayer engages the Christian 'I' in a particular and unique way, thereby defining and determining the 'I' in the way that the prayer is heard and responded to.

It is surely no accident that Lohmeyer worked on this book during his military service in the Second World War. Anyone involved in active military service in war-time must realistically consider the possibility of being killed. If Lohmeyer took this possibility seriously, his work on the Lord's Prayer meant that he was making a statement about his own beliefs, and what he believed Christianity in its earliest form to be about. The book also enabled him to make a statement about his view of the relationship between the 'Jesus of history' and the traditions of the earliest Church, which Lohmeyer had spent a lifetime of scholarship

---

[190] *Vater-unser*, p.211, ET p.296.

elucidating. The book ends with a ringing testimony to that view:

> The Lord's Prayer witnesses to an historical and factual mediation between the Synoptic and Johannine traditions, grounded in the preaching of Jesus, between the Synoptic Gospels and the Gospel of John. It has taken more its words and form from the former, its spirit and content from the latter, but has formed from both a unique unity which differs from both, but is contained in its own cell-like fullness, which promises many developments ... The Lord's Prayer is not only the most complete prayer, the like of which no other religion has yet produced; it is incomparably the prayer of Christianity, but it is also the supreme clear and great testimony to that which Jesus historically performed and proclaimed.[191]

It is clear from Lohmeyer's other writings, in his comments, for example, on the prayers prayed by Paul at the beginning of his letters (see above pp.106-7), that he regarded prayer to be the centre of Christian experience and, as Hönigswald had said, that it was what put into practice the theory of faith.

---

[191] *Vater-unser*, p.212-3, 'Das Vater-unser ist das Zeugnis für eine in Jesu Verkündung gegebene geschichtliche und sachliche Mitte zwischen der synoptischen und johanneischen Tradition, dem synoptischen und dem johanneischen Evangelium. Es hat von jenem mehr das Wort und die Form, vom diesem den Geist und Gehalt, und hat über beides hinaus eine ursprüngliche Einheit, welche sich von beiden scheidet und sicher in ihren eigenen keimhaften, alle Entfaltungen verheißenden Fülle wohnt ... das Vater-unser [ist] nicht nur das volkommene Gebet, dem keine andere Religion bisher an die Seite zu setzen hat, das darum das Gebet der Christenheit schlechthin ist, sondern auch das klare und große Zeugnis, dessen, was Jesus geschichtlich gewirkt und verkündet hat.' (My translation). See pp.298-9 for the English translation of the book.

CHAPTER FOURTEEN

The Lecture on Myth: The Case for Ernst Lohmeyer

In the April and June of 1941, Rudolf Bultmann delivered a lecture to the Society for Evangelical Theology, entitled, 'The New Testament and Mythology'. The society had been established in 1940 to oppose the politics of the Nazi régime; and the lecture was published in the collection *Kerygma and Myth*.[192] It sparked off the debate about demythologising and Lohmeyer was invited to contribute to this debate. This he did on 9 January 1944 in Breslau in a lecture entitled, 'The Right Interpretation of the Mythological'.[193] It was, and remains, a remarkable lecture, bringing together all of Lohmeyer's philosophical and religious views with remarkable clarity. It is arguably the greatest testimony to his genius, and an achievement that underlines how grievous it was that he was lost to biblical scholarship after 1946.

It is not my purpose to outline the content of Bultmann's lecture. Rather, I shall try to present Lohmeyer's criticisms in such a way that the central issues raised by Bultmann become clear, as does the alternative approach proposed by Lohmeyer.

---

[192] See K. Hammann, *Rudolf Bultmann. Eine Biographie*, Tübingen: Mohr Siebeck, 2007, pp.308-313. R. Bultmann, 'New Testament and Mythology', in H. W. Bartsch, *Kerygma and Myth*, London: SPCK, 1964, pp.1-44.

[193] E. Lohmeyer, 'Die rechte Interpretation des Mythologischen', in H. W. Bartsch, *Kerygma und Mythos*, Hamburg: Herbert Reich Ev. Verlag, 1948, pp.154-165; reprinted in W. Otto (ed.), *Freiheit in der Gebundenheit*, pp.18-35, to which reference is here made. For the English, see *Kerygma and Myth*, vol. 1, pp.124-137.

Lohmeyer began by placing Bultmann's lecture in the context of discussions about interpreting the mythological since the rise of critical scholarship. The Enlightenment, in its quest for 'pure reason', had regarded myths as narratives which contained truths that needed to be extracted from their supernatural trimmings. The trimmings, or forms of the myths, could be discounted once the essential content had been extracted. German Idealist philosophy (Lohmeyer mentioned Hegel) had altered the discussion by proposing to establish philosophically the metaphysical realities that myths spoke of or implied. This was also a type of demythologising, in that it separated the form from the content of myths and represented them in terms of speculative philosophy. Bultmann had moved the debate in a new direction. The process of interpretation was now determined by the philosophy of Existentialism, and the essential content of myths was re-expressed in terms of Existentialism. This also did violence to myths by separating form from content. Myths spoke of God and the gods, while Existentialism spoke of human existence.

Bultmann had defined myth in a 'history of religions' way as narratives in which supernatural, divine and eternal matters were presented as occurrences in the historical and human worlds. This was not incorrect in itself. There was no other way in which the divine and supernatural could be spoken of; but by separating the form of myths from their content, Bultmann's method silenced all religions and reduced their claims about reality to nothingness.

The first way out of the problem was to recognise that myths did not speak simply about the relation of God to humanity, so that they could be reduced to statements about human existence. Myths spoke of the relation of God and the gods to the world, its stars, its underworld. In the New Testament, the accounts of the miracles and healings of Jesus were mythical in form. The interpretation had to treat the narratives as a whole. To disentangle form from content was difficult and destructive.[194]

Lohmeyer next took issue with Bultmann's assertion that it belonged to the nature of myths themselves that they should be demythologised. This was not wrong as such, but it was wrong if it assumed that myths only spoke of human existence as conceived in humanistic terms; but they did not. Myths placed human existence in cosmic contexts and in relation to beyond-human powers. Myths described the limitations of human life and achievements. They also made claims about the nature of the divine and the relation of the divine to the

---

[194] Lohmeyer's lecture on myth was one of the earliest contributions to a debate that continued for many years after his murder, and in the light of which Bultmann's position came to be seen more positively than Lohmeyer understood it at the time. My friend and former colleague Andrew Lincoln has kindly supplied the following observations: 'As I understand it, a more sympathetic reading finds that Bultmann's demythologising has two dialectical aspects – the negative one of a critique of ancient world-pictures, and the positive one of translating their kerygma into new contexts. It distinguishes form (myth) from content (kerygma), but does not divorce them. The kerygma – God's eschatological address to humans – always takes a cultural form and so needs to be re-contextualised or re-mythologised in new settings. "Existential interpretation" for Bultmann is not being determined by a philosophy of Existentialism or reducing everything to the human realm, but an insistence that the kerygma must directly address the human existential situation. This is why it seems strange today for Lohmeyer to say that Bultmann wanted to separate theology from preaching. Bultmann's programme of demythologising was precisely aimed at proclamation, at showing that God's address to humans should not become objectified but continue to provide a disruptive existential encounter. The sermon was the vehicle for just such an encounter. On this view perhaps Lohmeyer and Bultmann were not so far apart as Lohmeyer seemed to think. For all his emphasis on not separating form and content, Lohmeyer, in translating the message of the text for a contemporary setting, inevitably was involved in doing that. Bultmann wanted to expose the radical nature of the necessity of such translation, but without abandoning God-talk or reducing it to the merely human.'

world, and it was not adequate to describe God as simply 'the ground of being'. The New Testament claimed that 'God so loved the world'. It claimed that the world and humanity came from, and rested in the hand of God. Myths drew their form and content from the inexhaustible threefold constellation of theological, cosmological and anthropological grounds. They combined to define human existence in deeper ways than that offered by Existentialism.

Bultmann, according to Lohmeyer, wanted to separate theology from preaching or proclamation, with the latter being the province of the pulpit. For Lohmeyer, this distinction rested upon a false understanding of the nature of theology, and also made the fatal mistake of assuming that what was proclaimed was not 'scientific' or open to critical scrutiny. The purpose of Christian proclamation was to invoke faith, and the proclamation that did this was mythical in the sense that it spoke of God, heaven, and salvation, among other things. The proclamation was also presented in historical terms in the New Testament. The Word had become flesh. The task of theology was to position what was proclaimed into a systematic scheme of comprehension, that did full justice to what was proclaimed and to the belief that it engendered and was necessary to the whole matter.

Lohmeyer repeatedly insisted on the need for a 'believing theology', and it is at this point that his indebtedness to Hönigswald becomes most apparent. For any discipline to be scientific, its concepts had to be open to epistemological examination; but the method of examination had to be appropriate to the discipline involved. It was noted earlier that Hönigswald had disagreed fundamentally with those Neo-Kantians who wished to make mathematics the sole methodology from which to evaluate all academic disciplines (p.23). For Lohmeyer, it was necessary for theology to be scientific, but the philosophy – or perhaps one should say the epistemology that guaranteed its scientific status – had to be appropriate to its subject matter, essential to which was belief as a defining fact of human identity.

Existential philosophy, as such, was not equipped to pass judgement on theology. Philosophy, generally speaking (and perhaps we should add, as defined by Hönigswald), could be described as follows:

> Its function is ... of a methodological or logical nature, and therewith it embraces theology, as for instance it does natural science. But on the actual subject matter of theology it has no more right to pontificate than it has to do with physics, and it makes no difference whether the philosophy is Existentialism, or naturalism, or idealism, or materialism. It may be true that Existentialist philosophy arrives in the end at statements almost identical with those of Christian theology, but this is not because it is a philosophy, but because it borrows its thesis from other spheres which belong to another kingdom and another order.[195]

Immanuel Kant had famously written in his *Critique of Pure Reason* that 'thoughts without concepts are empty; intuitions without content are blind'.[196] Lohmeyer parodied this, saying:

---

[195] 'Die rechte Interpretation', p .30, 'Ihre Funktion ist also methodischer oder logischer Art, und mit ihr umfaßt sie auch das Gefüge der Theologie wie etwa das der Naturwissenschaft. Aber innerhalb des Bereiches, den der Gegenstand der Theologie umgrenzt, hat sie ebensowenig Recht mitzusprechen wie im Bereiche der Physik, und es ist dabei gleich, ob es sich um eine existentielle oder naturalistische, um eine idealistische oder um eine materialistische Philosophie handelt. Wohl mag es sein, dass die Existentialphilosophie zu ähnlichen Aussagen kommt wie die christliche Theologie, aber dann tut sie es nicht, weil sie Philosophie ist, sondern weil sie ihre Thesen aus anderen Bezirken nimmt, die nicht ihres Reiche und ihrer Art sind.'

[196] I. Kant, *Kritik der reinen Vernunft* 2. Auflage, 1787 in *Kants Werke Akademie Textausgabe*, Berlin: de Gruyter, 1968, Bd. III, p.75, 'Gedanken ohne Inhalt sind leer; Anschauungen ohne Begriffe sind blind'. ET *Immanuel Kant's Critique of*

'Without believing theology all scientific theology is empty, and without scientific theology all believing theology is blind'.[197] What he meant by this was as follows. There would be no such thing as a theology in the first place if faith were not engendered, and engendered by a tradition in mythological form and with mythological elements. Therefore, a theology that claimed to be scientific, but which ignored the faith which the traditions engendered, would be empty, and would have no content appropriate to the believing theology. On the other hand, a theology that started from or with the faith engendered by the tradition, but ignored the need for it to be understood and articulated in scientific terms (the German *wissenschaftlich* is much broader than the English 'scientific' and closer in meaning to 'scholarly, critical, and academic'), would be blind, that is, cut off from being one of many scientific disciplines that could be subjected to critical historical examination and epistemological critique. Bultmann, in effect, wanted his theology to be scientific, something for which Lohmeyer commended him,[198] but he did so in a way that destroyed or totally altered the indissoluble unity of form and content of the mythical-type traditions that engendered the faith that gave birth to theology. The task of New Testament interpretation was not to destroy and secularise the mythology in the tradition, but to seek to interpret it while taking full account of the historical form and circumstance in which it was given, the experience of faith which had engendered it, and the way that faith could be positioned within a scientific philosophy (which for Lohmeyer was that

Pure Reason (trans. N. Kemp Smith), London: Macmillan, 1968, p.93.
[197] 'Die rechte Interpretation'. p.32, 'Alle wissenschaftliche Theologie ohne gläubige Theologie ist leer, alle gläubige Theologie ohne wissenschaftliche Theologie ist blind'.
[198] 'Die rechte Interpretation', p.25, 'Damit wäre der Gedanke einer wissenschaftichen Theologie preisgegeben, der doch Bultmann so stark, wie wenigen, am Herzen liegt', ET, p.129.

of Hönigswald). Lohmeyer's closing paragraph sums up all this succinctly:

> To have its faith tried and tested in the fires of doubt is of the very essence of Protestant theology ... but it knows that the act of God which is the ground of its own experience is greater than myth, and that it can experience this act more genuinely the more it penetrates behind mythology to the essential core of truth. Protestant theology knows that myth is the mode in which God has chosen to reveal himself. That revelation is a treasure which we have to bear in earthen vessels, not only because we are men of earth, but because it has pleased God to place it in this vessel. It is not for us to smash the vessel, but to make proper use of it and to learn that after all it is an earthen vessel.[199]

I propose to conclude this chapter and the book by describing an imaginary discussion between Bultmann and Lohmeyer regarding the interpretation of the Parable of the Lost Sheep and the Parable of the Lost Coin in Luke 15.3-10. It is possible, of course, that I shall misrepresent both of them; but it will enable me to give an account of how I have come to understand Lohmeyer, and what I think the challenge is that he still presents to biblical scholars. The Parable of the Lost Sheep does, of course, also occur at Matthew 18:10-14, but Lohmeyer's commentary on Matthew has a gap at this point and we do not know what he would have said about it there.[200]

---

[199] 'Die rechte Interpretation', pp.34-5, 'An dem Zweifel den festen Grund zu finden, im Glauben auch noch die Anfechtung zu tragen, gehört zu ihrem [dem Protestantismus] Wesen ... [er] weiß auch, dass es Gott gefallen hat, eben in dem Mythos sich zu offenbaren. Wir tragen auch diesen Schatz in irdischen Gefäßen – nicht nur weil wir irdisch sind, sondern weil Gott ihn in diese Gefäße gefüllt hat. Uns ist nicht gegeben, ja uns ist es genommen, diese Gefäße zu zerbrechen, aber uns ist es auch aufgegeben zu erkennen, dass diese Gefäße irdisch sind.'

[200] Lohmeyer, *Matthäusevangelium*, p.277 note ** (sic).

The two parables contain mythological elements, that is, elements that speak of things beyond the world of time and space. Luke 15.7 speaks of the joy in heaven over one sinner who repents, while Luke 15.10 speaks of joy before the angels of God over one sinner's repentance. The mythological elements are thus God, angels and heaven, and there are also mythological elements in the words 'sinner' and 'repents' because they imply a status and a relationship between humans or a human and God, which is of significance not just within, but beyond the world of time and space.

> 1 Then drew near unto him all the publicans and sinners for to hear him.
> 2 And the Pharisees and scribes murmured, saying, This man receiveth sinners, and eateth with them.
> 3 And he spake this parable unto them, saying,
> 4 What man of you, having an hundred sheep, if he lose one of them, doth not leave the ninety and nine in the wilderness, and go after that which is lost, until he find it?
> 5 And when he hath found *it*, he layeth *it* on his shoulders, rejoicing.
> 6 And when he cometh home, he calleth together *his* friends and neighbours, saying unto them, Rejoice with me; for I have found my sheep which was lost.
> 7 I say unto you, that likewise joy shall be in heaven over one sinner that repenteth, more than over ninety and nine just persons, which need no repentance.
> 8 Either what woman having ten pieces of silver, if she lose one piece, doth not light a candle, and sweep the house, and seek diligently till she find *it*?
> 9 And when she hath found *it*, she calleth *her* friends and *her* neighbours together, saying, Rejoice with me; for I have found the piece which I had lost.
> 10 Likewise, I say unto you, there is joy in the presence of the angels of God over one sinner that repenteth.

An important element in my creation of the imaginary dialogue is the interpretation of the parables in Oliver Quick's book *The Realism of Christ's Parables*.[201] Quick draws attention to the way in which losing and finding are things that happen universally, and argues that Jesus, in linking these human experiences with divine reality, 'unveil[s] something of the mystery of the Kingdom in facts which are genuinely commonplace',[202] and that parables, like the life of Jesus, 'bring what is really divine down to what is genuinely common-place, and in so doing lift the commonplace towards heaven'.[203] I see, rightly or wrongly, something in these words that Lohmeyer would have endorsed, especially the unveiling of the mystery of the Kingdom, and the mutual relationship between the really divine and the genuinely commonplace. Quick also comes near to Lohmeyer's view, expressed in the Matthew commentary and the essay upon parables (see p.158), that parables are events that embody and proclaim the Kingdom. A further, and crucial, point is that Quick shows that these particular parables can engender faith when people are moved from their own joy in finding a lost object to experiencing how God feels about people turning to him.

A demythologising interpretation of the parables, such as I am ascribing to Bultmann, would have to say that the mytho-logical elements, that is, the angels, heaven and perhaps even God, belong to a pre-scientific understanding of the world that is no longer viable today. A genuine experience of encounter could be acknowledged, that is, of sharing in the universal experience of joy at finding a lost object; but this would need to be restated in humanistic terms, such as a realisation of a person's oneness with others in certain human experiences. The horizon of the demythologising interpretation would be confined to the world of time and space.

---

[201] O.C. Quick, *The Realism of Christ's Parables*, London: SCM Press, 1937, pp. 29-31.
[202] Quick, *Realism*, p.30
[203] Quick, *Realism*, p.31

An interpretation along the lines of Lohmeyer would take the faith encounter seriously, and would see the mythological elements in the parables as indispensable to making the faith encounter possible. Without them, we merely have two stories about people being happy after finding something lost. Another element, not so far mentioned, is that in both stories, the finder shares the joy of the finding with friends and neighbours, and it is this spontaneous desire to celebrate with others that points towards the joy in heaven. In Lohmeyer's terms, the faith encounter made possible by reading or hearing the parables needs to be accounted for as an aspect of human experience, and in order for this to be done, a view of reality is needed that is appropriate to the faith experience and its situatedness in mythological ideas. Lohmeyer found this view of reality in Hönigswald's philosophy, with its insistence that a philosophy that adequately describes the 'I'-relatedness of encounter with objects had to give autonomy to aesthetic and religious experiences.

This did not necessarily make Lohmeyer an orthodox Christian believer in the sense that he accepted as meta-physical realities the statements made in the traditional creeds about the nature of Christ as human and divine. I do not know what Lohmeyer thought about such matters, except to say that I am certain that he believed in God as encountered in the New Testament traditions, that he prayed to God and that he interpreted his own life in terms of the eschatological purpose that he believed to have been disclosed in the preaching and suffering of Jesus as the Son of Man. But he was a Protestant theologian, not a Catholic one, and he accepted that in some sense demythologising had to be part of Protestant theology[204]

---

[204] 'Die rechte Interpretation', p.34, 'Sie [die protestantische Theologie] kann ... der Forderung der Entmythologisieren nicht grundsätzlich sich verschließen, wie es etwa ein katholischer Glaube tun könnte und tat', English, p.136.

in a way that might not be possible for Catholics. One senses, especially in the classic essay on Philippians 2.5-11, a reluctance on the part of Lohmeyer to commit himself to an interpretation of the nature of Jesus in traditional orthodox Christian terms, which may be why he was so much criticised by scholars who otherwise acknowledged their indebtedness to him.

Let me suggest how a Lohmeyer commentary on the Parables of the Lost Sheep and Lost Coin might have looked. First, great attention would be paid to the historical and social setting: the nature of being a shepherd in Palestine at the time of Jesus; why a sheep might be lost; and the danger from wild animals and robbers faced by the lost sheep and by the flock, temporarily abandoned during the search. In the case of the woman who had lost the coin it would be the nature of what was lost that would be discussed. Was it valuable, was it part of her bridal-wealth, a security if she was divorced? What would a Palestinian house be like that needed to be swept with the help of a lamp? Also, the presence of one of the parables in Matthew's Gospel would perhaps have prompted Lohmeyer to locate its origin in memories of Galilean 'poor' Christian circles, in spite of the Lucan location of the story. Links with John 10.1-18 would surely have been suggested, while the seemingly irrational behaviour of the shepherd in abandoning his ninety-nine sheep to seek the one lost would have pointed to parallels such as the extravagant and irrational behaviour of the woman with costly ointment in Mark 14.3-9.

Above all – and how this would have been expressed, if at all, I cannot say – Lohmeyer would have been influenced by his conviction that the mythical or mythological elements in the stories had to be taken seriously, not in the sense that they made it obligatory for him to believe in God, angels, heaven and sinners in the exact way in which they were mentioned in the parables, but as being necessary to the faith experience the parables could engender. The parable spoke of realities that transcended the closed world, and which defined human existence and experience in metaphysical ways, even if the metaphysics could not be articulated in terms of German idealistic philosophy or even traditional Christian formularies. Yet what remained real were faith, hope and love, deriving from God, who was experienced as the Unconditioned in the commonplace language of the parable, and who was addressed in prayer and was served in a committed life.

The challenge, and thus the case for Lohmeyer, is this. Can biblical interpretation be done without some type of philosophy that takes seriously that dimension of human experience that includes aesthetics and religious belief? The answer is obviously 'yes', if the Biblical Studies involved are restricted to such things as textual criticism, the sociology of religion, biblical geography and history, or cultural studies. The answer is obviously 'yes', if, in dealing with biblical narratives, God is regarded merely as a character in a narrative text, with no extra-textual reference. But the answer is surely 'no' if biblical interpretation is to do justice to the truth claims implicit in the text, truth claims about the nature and origin of the world, the nature of humanity and the destiny of both. Perversely, it might be claimed that only by ignoring such things can Biblical Studies be truly academic or scientific and can preserve its objectivity from the distortions of a faith commitment. Yet Lohmeyer's quest was for Biblical Studies to be 'scientific' in the sense that all academic disciplines needed to be scientific, whether physics, chemistry, biology, botany or the like. Only in this way could Biblical Studies, theology and other humanities take their rightful place in universities, and only in this way could universities claim to represent completely and adequately the total endeavour of humanity to seek for truth and enlightenment.

It may well be that in some, or even many, details of historical and literary scholarship, Lohmeyer was wrong. His propensity for discerning patterns and literary structures in terms of sevens and threes, his insistence upon the apocalyptic Son of Man figure as the clue to the mission and message of Jesus, his understanding of Paul's letters in terms of impending martyrdom, his refusal to accept standard views of the literary relationship of the Synoptic Gospels – all of these may well have contained exaggerations, which distanced him from his colleagues and which resulted in his posthumous neglect. Yet his basic convictions were surely correct: Biblical Studies and Theology must be scientific, which meant finding ways of taking seriously the truth claims implicit and explicit in their traditions. In carrying out this programme so single-mindedly and often in such an individualistic way, Lohmeyer produced countless exhilarating insights and interpretations that have not lost their power to excite and challenge those prepared to grapple with his voluminous and often formidable writings. The harvest is plenteous, but the labourers are few. This book will have been worthwhile if it persuades more labourers to venture into that harvest, and to convey its produce to others.

Memorial plaque at the University of Greifswald

Bibliography

The following bibliography lists the books and articles used in preparation for the present book. A full bibliography of Lohmeyer's published works is given in **A. Köhn**, *Der Neutestamentler Ernst Lohmeyer*, pp.342-351.

Barrett, C. K., *The Acts of the Apostles*, (International Critical Commentary), Edinburgh: T. & T. Clark, vol. 2, 1998

Beiser, F. C., *The Fate of Reason. German Philosophy from Kant to Fichte*, Cambridge, Mass.: Harvard University Press, 1987

Birus, H., K. Eibl, (eds.), 'Gedichte, West-Östlicher Divan', in F. Apel *et al.* (eds.), *Goethe Werke Jubiläumsausgabe*, vol. 1, Darmstadt: Wissenshaftliche Buchgesellschaft, 1998

Bonnard, P., *L'Épître de Saint Paul aux Philippiens* (Commentaire du Nouveau Testament X), Neuchâtel: Delachaux et Niestlé, 1950

Breil, R., *Hönigswald und Kant*, Bonn: Bouvier Verlag, 1991

Bultmann, R., 'New Testament and Mythology', in H. W. Bartsch, *Kerygma and Myth*, London: SPCK, 1964, pp.1-44

Bultmann, R., *The History of the Synoptic Tradition*, trans. J. Marsh, Oxford: Blackwell, 1968

Charles, R. H., *A Critical and Exegetical Commentary on the Revelation of St John* (International Critical Commentary), Edinburgh: T. & T. Clark, 1920

Copleston, F., *A History of Philosophy, vol. 7, Modern Philosophy Part II: Schopenhauer to Nietzsche*, New York: Image Books, 1965, Part 2

Dodd, C. H., *The Parables of the Kingdom*, London: Nisbet, 1935

Esking, E., *Glaube und Geschichte in der theologischen Exegese Ernst Lohmeyers. Zugleich ein Beitrag zur Geschichte der neutestamentlichen Interpretation* (Acta seminarii neotestamentica upsaliensis ebenda curavit A. Fridrichsen XVIII), Copenhagen: Ejnar Munksgaard; Lund: Gleerups, 1951

Eusebius von Caesarea, *Kirchengeschichte*, trans P. Häuser, Munich: Kösel Verlag, 1981

Freyne, S., 'Galilee (Hellenistic/Roman)' in *Anchor Bible Dictionary,* vol. 2, pp.895-899

George, S., *Der siebente Ring,* Berlin: Georg Bondi, 1914

George, S., *Das neue Reich,* Berlin: Georg Bondi, 1928

Gnilka, J., *Das Matthäusevangelium. 2. Teil 14, 1-28, 20,* Darmstadt: Wissenschaftliche Buchgesellschaft, 2000

Gnilka, J., *Der Kolosserbrief* (Herders Theologischer Kommentar zum Neuen Testament), Freiburg: Herder Verlag, 2002

Goethe, J. W. von, *Faust,* edited by A. E. Schöne, Frankfurt: Deutsche Klassiker Verlag, 1994

Grassl, R., *Der junge Richard Hönigswald. Eine biographisch fundierte Kontextualisierung in historischer Absicht* (Studien und Materialen zum Neukantianismus 13), Würzburg: Königshausen & Neumann, 1998

Gundolf, F., *George,* Berlin: Georg Bondi, 1930, 3rd edition of the 1920 book

Hamacher, B., *Johann Wolfgang von Goethe. Entwürfe eines Lebens,* Darmstadt: Wissenschaftliche Buchgesellschaft, 2010

Hammann, K., *Rudolf Bultmann. Eine Biographie,* Tübingen: Mohr Siebeck, 2007

Heselhaus, C., *Deutsche Lyrik der Moderne von Nietzsche bis Yvan Goll,* Düsseldorf: August Bagel Verlag, 1961

Holz, H. H., edited by J. Zimmer *Leibniz. Das Lebenswerk eines Universalgelehrten,* Darmstadt: Wissenschaftliche Buchgesellschaft, 2013

Hönigswald, R., *Erkenntnistheoretisches zur Schöpfungsgeschichte der Genesis,* Sammlung Gemeinverständliche Vorträge und Schriften aus dem Gebiet der Theologie und Religionsgeschichte 161, Tübingen: J. C. B. Mohr, 1932

Hönigswald, R., *Grundfragen der Erkenntnistheorie,* Tübingen: J.C.B. Mohr (Paul Siebeck), 1931

Hutter, U., 'Theologie als Wissenschaft. Zu Leben und Werk Ernst Lohmeyers (1890-1946). Mit einem Quellenanhang', *Jahrbuch für Schlesische Kirchengeschichte* 69 (1990), pp.123-169

Jüngel, E., *Paulus und Jesus. Eine Untersuchung zur Präzisierung der Frage nach dem Ursprung der Christologie* (Hermeneutische

Untersuchungen zur Theologie 2), Tübingen: Mohr Siebeck, 2004 (7th ed.)

Kant, I., 'Kritik der reinen Vernunft 2'. Auflage, 1787 in *Kants Werke Akademie Textausgabe,* Berlin: de Gruyter, 1968, Bd. III; ET *Immanuel Kant's Critique of Pure Reason* (trans. N. Kemp Smith), London: Macmillan, 1968

Käsemann, E., 'Kritische Analyse von Phil. 2.5-11', *Zeitschrift für Theologie und Kirche* 47 (1950) pp.313-360

Kee, H. C., 'The Testaments of the Twelve Patriarchs' in J. H. Charlesworth (ed.), *The Old Testament Pseudepigrapha. Vol. 1, Apocalyptic Literature and Testaments,* New York: Doubleday, 1983

Köhn, A., *Der Neutestamentler Ernst Lohmeyer. Studien zu Biographie und Theologie.* (Wissenschaftliche Untersuchungen zum Neuen Testament 2), Reihe 180, Tübingen: Mohr Siebeck, 2004

Kosian, J., 'Richard Hönigswalds Denkpsychologie` in E.O. Orth, D. Aleksandrowicz (eds.), *Studien zur Philosophie Richard Hönigswalds* (Studien und Materialen zum Neukantianismus 7), Würzburg: Königshausen & Neumann, 1996, pp.37-48

Kuhn, D., *Metaphysik und Geschichte. Zur Theologie Ernst Lohmeyers.* (Theologische Bibliothek Töpelmann, 131), Berlin: De Gruyter, 2005

Kutsch, E., *Neues Testament – Neuer Bund? Eine Fehlübersetzung wird korrigiert.* Neukirchen-Vluyn: Neukirchener Verlag, 1978

Laub, F., 'Philipperbrief' in *Neues Bibel Lexikon,* vol. 4, pp.137-8

Lessing, G. E., *Die Erziehung des Menschengeschlechts* in *Gotthold Ephraim Lessing Werke,* Darmstadt: Wissenschaftliche Buch-gesellschaft, 1996, vol. 8, p.500; ET, by F. W. Robertson, London: Anthroposophical Publishing Co., 1927

Lohmeyer, E., *Diatheke. Ein Beitrag zur Erklärung des neutestamentlichen Begriffs* (*Untersuchungen zum Neuen Testament*), Hans Windisch (ed.), Leipzig: J. C. Heinrichs'sche Buchhandlung, 1913

Lohmeyer, E., *Soziale Fragen im Urchristentum*, Leipzig: Wissenschaft und Bildung 172, 1921. Photographic reprint, Darmstadt: Wissenschaftliche Buchgesellschaft, 1973

Lohmeyer, E., *Vom Begriff der religiösen Gemeinschaft*, in R. Hönigswald (ed.), *Wissenschaftliche Grundfragen. Philosophische Abhandlungen* III, Leipzig: Verlag B. G. Teubner, 1925

Lohmeyer, E., *Die Offenbarung des Johannes* (Handbuch zum Neuen Testament 16), Tübingen: J. C. B. Mohr (Paul Siebeck), 1926

Lohmeyer, E., *Kyrios Jesus. Eine Untersuchung zu Phil. 2, 5-11.* Sitzungsberichte der Heidelberger Akademie der Wissenschaften, Philosophisch-historische Klasse, Jhrg. 1927/28, 4. Abhandlung. 2nd edition, Heidelberg: Carl Winter, 1961

Lohmeyer, E., 'Kritische und Gestaltende Prinzipien im Neuen Testament' in P. Tillich, (ed.), *Protestantismus als Kritik und Gestaltung*, Darmstadt: Otto Reich Verlag, 1929, pp.41-69

Lohmeyer, E., *Grundlagen paulinischer Theologie* (Beiträge zur historischen Theologie 1), Tübingen: J. C. B. Mohr (Paul Siebeck), 1929

Lohmeyer, E., *Die Briefe an die Philipper, an die Kolosser und an Philemon* (Kritisch-exegetischer Kommentar über das Neue Testament), Göttingen: Vandenhoeck & Ruprecht, 1930

Lohmeyer, E., *Glaube und Geschichte in vorderorientalischen Religionen. Rede gehalten bei der Einführung in das Rektorat am 3. November 1930*, Breslauer Universitätsreden Heft 6, Breslau: Ferdinand Hirt, 1931

Lohmeyer, E., *Das Urchristentum. 1. Buch. Johannes der Täufer*, Göttingen: Vandenhoeck & Ruprecht, 1932

Lohmeyer, E., *Galiläa und Jerusalem* (Forschungen zur Religion und Literatur des Alten und Neuen Testaments, Neue Folge 34), Göttingen: Vandenhoeck & Ruprecht, 1936

Lohmeyer, E., *Das Evangelium des Markus* (Kritisch-exegetischer Kommentar über das Neue Testament), Göttingen: Vandenhoeck & Ruprecht, 1937

Lohmeyer, E., 'Vom Sinn der Gleichnisse Jesu' in *Zeitschrift für systematische Theologie* 15 (1938) pp.319-346, reprinted in: **Lohmeyer, E.**, *Urchristliche Mystok. Neutestamentliche Studien*, Darmstadt: Wissenschaftliche Buchgesellschaft, 1958, pp.123-157

Lohmeyer, E., *Kultus und Evangelium*, Göttingen: Kommissionsverlag Vandenhoeck & Ruprecht, 1942

Lohmeyer, E., *Das Vater-unser*, Göttingen: Vandenhoeck & Ruprecht, 1946, pp.194-5; ET *The Lord's Prayer*, London: Collins, 1965, pp.274-5

Lohmeyer, E., 'Die rechte Interpretation des Mythologischen', in H. W. Bartsch, *Kerygma und Mythos*, Hamburg: Herbert Reich Ev. Verlag, 1948, pp.154-165; reprinted in W. Otto (ed.), *Freiheit in der Gebundenheit*, pp.18-35; ET 'The Right Interpretation of the Mythical' in H. W. Bartsch, *Kerygma and Myth. A Theological Debate* (translated by R. H. Fuller), London: SPCK, 1964, pp.124-136

Lohmeyer, E., *Probleme paulinischer Theologie*, Stuttgart: Kohlhammer Verlag, 1955

Lohmeyer, E., (ed. W. Schmauch), *Das Evangelium des Matthäus* (Kritisch-exegetischer Kommentar über das Neue Testament), Göttingen: Vandenhoeck & Ruprecht, 1956

Lohse, E., *Die Texte aus Qumran*, Munich: Kösel Verlag, 1964

Luz, U., *Das Evangelium nach Matthäus* (Mt. 8-17), Zürich: Benzinger Verlag; Neukirchen-Vluyn: Neukirchener Verlag, 1990

Martin, R. P., *Carmen Christi. Philippians ii.5-11 in Recent Interpretation and in the Setting of Early Christian Worship*, Cambridge: Cambridge University Press, 1967

Marx, O. and E. Morwitz (trans.), *The Works of Stefan George. Rendered into English*, Chapel Hill: University of North Carolina Press, 2nd edition, 1974

Morwitz, E., *Kommentar zu dem Werk Stefan Georges*, Munich and Düsseldorf: Helmut Küpper vormals Georg Bondi, 1960

Orth, E. O. and D. Aleksandrowicz (eds.), *Studien zur Philosophie Richard Hönigswalds* (Studien und Materialen zum Neukantianismus 7), Würzburg: Königshausen & Neumann, 1996

Otto, W., (ed.), *Freiheit in der Gebundenheit. Zur Erinnerung an den Theologen Ernst Lohmeyer anläßlich seines 100. Geburtstages,* Göttingen: Vandenhoeck & Reuprecht, 1990

Otto, W., (ed.), *Aus der Einsamkeit – Briefe einer Freundschaft. Richard Hönigswald an Ernst Lohmeyer,* Würzburg: Königshausen und Neumann, 1999

Quick, O. C., *The Realism of Christ's Parables,* London: SCM Press, 1937

Ranke, L. von, *Über die Epochen der neuen Geschichte. Vorträge dem Könige Maximillan II von Bayern,* Historische-kritische Ausgabe, ed. T. Schedig, Munich: H. Bentung, 1971

Rawlinson, A. E. J., *The Gospel according to St Mark* (Westminster Commentaries), London: Methuen, 1925

Rogerson, J. W., *Myth in Old Testament Interpretation* (Beihefte zur Zeitschrift für die alttestamentliche Wissenschaft 134) Berlin: De Gruyter, 1974

Salin, E., *Um Stefan George.* Godesberg: Verlag Helmut Küpper, 1948

Schlüssler, W., E. Sturm, *Paul Tillich, Leben-Werk-Wirkung,* Darmstadt: Wissenschaftliche Buchgesellschaft, 2007

Schmauch, W., *In Memoriam Ernst Lohmeyer,* Stuttgart: Evangelisches Verlagswerk, 1951

Schmied-Kowarzik, W. (ed.), *Erkennen – Monas – Sprache. Internationales Richard-Hönigswald-Symposium, Kassel 1995,* Würzburg: Königshausen & Neumann, 1997

Schnabel, T., 'Das Neue Reich.' Der Dichter Stefan George und die Brüder Stauffenberg, *Momente. Beiträge zur Landeskunde von Baden-Württemberg* 4 (2006), pp.8-11

Scholder, K., *Die Kirchen und das Dritte Reich. I Vorgeschichte und Zeit der Illusion 1918-1934*, Munich: Prophäen Taschenbuch, 2004

Schönauer, F., *Stefan George in Selbstzeugnissen und Bilddokumenten*. Reinbek-bei-Hamburg: Rowohlt Verlag, 1969

Stevenson, J., *A New Eusebius*, London: SPCK, 1957

Tillich, P., (ed.), *Protestantismus als Kritik und Gestaltung*, Darmstadt: Otto Reich Verlag, 1929

Vermes, G., *The Complete Dead Sea Scrolls in English*, London: Allen Lane, 1992

Weber, C., *Altes Testament und völkische Frage: Der biblische Volksbegriff in der alttestamentlichen Wissenschaft der national-sozialistischen Zeit, dargestellt am Beispiel von Johannes Hempel (1891-1964)*. (Forschungen zum Alten Testament 38), Tübingen: Mohr Siebeck, 2000

Winkler, M., *Stefan George*, Stuttgart: J. B. Metzler, 1970

Biblical References

Genesis

1	29, 72
3.5	85
15.6	50
31.43-54	44

Exodus

19.16	153
24.16	152
34.29	153

Numbers

6.1-6	145

Deuteronomy

10.8-9	45

I Samuel

18.1-4	44, 47

I Kings

17.9	130
22.17	162

Psalms

22	157
33.6	30

Isaiah

6.9-10	157
9.1-2	141
40.3	127
51.16-23	156
53	86, 88
55.3	47
61.1	151

Jeremiah

1.4	30
31.31-4	46, 49

Ezekiel

34	162

Daniel

7.5-7	78
7.13	86, 135

Hosea

1.1-3	46
6.7	46
8.1	46

Amos

3.2	46

Malachi

3.1	125

I Enoch

46.5	86
48.2	86

Matthew

1.14	136
3.10-11	129, 130
4.1-11	85
4.13-16	141
7.13-14	147
9.9	11
10.6	162
11.9	129
11.11	125
11.18-19	125
11.23	147
13.3-9	157
13.10-17	160
13.18-23	157-9
15.21-38	160, 162
23	142

Index

About the Author

J. W. ROGERSON

John William Rogerson was born in London in 1935 and educated at Bec School, Tooting, the Joint Services School for Linguists, Coulsdon Common, where he completed an intensive course in Russian, and the Universities of Manchester, Oxford and Jerusalem, where he studied Theology and Semitic Languages. Ordained in 1964, he served as Assistant Curate at St Oswald's, Durham. He was Lecturer (1964-1975) and then Senior Lecturer (1975-1979) in Theology at the University of Durham, before moving in 1979 to become Professor and Head of the Department of Biblical Studies at the University of Sheffield, retiring in 1996. He was made an honorary Canon of Sheffield Cathedral in 1982 and an Emeritus Canon in 1995.

As well as many essays and scholarly articles, Professor Rogerson's published books include: *Myth in Old Testament Interpretation* (1974); *Psalms* (Cambridge Bible Commentary, with J.W. McKay, 1977); *Anthropology and the Old Testament* (1978); *Old Testament Criticism in the Nineteenth Century: England and Germany* (1984); *New Atlas of the Bible* (1985, translated into nine languages); *W.M.L. de Wette, Founder of Modern Biblical Criticism. An Intellectual Biography* (1991); *The Bible and Criticism in Victorian Britain. Profiles of F.D. Maurice and William Robertson Smith* (1995); *Introduction to the Bible* (1999, 3rd edition 2012); *Eerdman's Commentary on the Bible* (joint editor with J.D.G. Dunn, 2000); *Nine o'Clock Service and Other Sermons* (2002); *Theory and Practice in Old Testament Ethics* (2004); *According to the Scriptures? The Challenge of Using the Bible in Social, Moral and Political Questions* (2007); *A Theology of the Old Testament. Cultural Memory, Communication and Being Human* (2009); *Strength in Weakness: The Scandal of the Cross* (2010); *The Art of Biblical Prayer* (2011); *More Places at the Table: Legal and Biblical Perspectives on Family Life* (with Imogen Clout, 2013); *Unexpected Discovery, Beauchief Abbey and Other Sermons* (2013); *On Being a Broad Church* (2013); *The Holy Spirit in Biblical and Pastoral Perspective* (2013); *Perspectives on the Passion* (2014); *Cultural Landscapes and the Bible: Collected Essays* (2015); *The Kingdom of God: Five Lectures* (2015).

Professor Rogerson received the degree of Doctor of Divinity for published work from the University of Manchester in 1975, an Honorary Degree of Doctor of Divinity from the University of Aberdeen, and an Honorary Degree of Dr.Theol. from the Friedrich-Schiller-Universität, Jena and from the Albert-Ludwigs-Universität, Freiburg-im-Breisgau.

Also by J.W. Rogerson

Published by Beauchief Abbey Press and available from www.lulu.com

CULTURAL LANDSCAPES
AND THE BIBLE (2014)

A collection of John Rogerson's essays, some in English translation for the first time, and many not readily accessible elsewhere. Topics covered range from anthropology and sociology (Section 1) to the history of interpretation (Section 2) and finally to the intersection of philosophy and theology (Section 3).

John Rogerson is an Old Testament scholar of amazing learning, versatility, and skill in exposition, notable also for his commitment to applying biblical insights to the demands of the modern world. This large volume consists of his most significant papers over a span of about 40 years.

John Barton, *Church Times*, 2015

Rogerson's essays will delight and provoke. His writing is engaging, his questions unrelenting, and his conclusions straightforwardly reasonable … A welcome contribution to biblical scholarship in both its breadth of scope and depth of insight.

Kurtis Peters, *The Expository Times*, January 2016

ON BEING A BROAD CHURCH (2013)

Professor Rogerson explores the social vision and work of the influential nineteenth-century Broad Church movement, led by writer Charles Kingsley and active campaigner and visionary churchman F. D. Maurice. This engaging series of lectures is here presented in a survey that reveals the importance of the Broad Church movement for contemporary Christian faith.

THE HOLY SPIRIT
IN BIBLICAL AND PASTORAL PERSPECTIVE (2013)

Language about the Holy Spirit in church worship is confused and contradictory. Professor Rogerson has put together a scholarly review of all biblical references to the Holy Spirit, and explores the implications for church teaching today, in order to help congregations, clergy and leaders navigate and understand the Church's perplexing language about the Holy Spirit.

PERSPECTIVES ON THE PASSION (2014)

How did the Early Church understand the Easter story? How has that understanding changed after two thousand years? What should we believe, and whom? This short book of public lectures and sermons explores the Church's differing perspectives on the meaning of Easter, and illuminates ways in which we can find thoughtful and active approaches to Easter today.